INSIDER'S PARIS
AN INTIMATE TOUR

Copyright © 2003, FILIPACCHI PUBLISHING, for the present edition
Copyright © 2003, EDITIONS FILIPACCHI, ELLE DÉCORATION, for the French edition

ISBN: 2-85018-670-8

Translated from French by Fern Malkine-Falvey
Edited by Jennifer Ditsler-Ladonne

Printed in France

The stores listed in the "Strolling" sections are meant to represent the spirit of an area and are by no means comprehensive.
At press time addresses were as up to date as possible, however in the meantime certain addresses may have changed.
The publisher cannot be held responsible for any inaccuracies.

INSIDER'S PARIS
AN INTIMATE TOUR

Jean Demachy - François Baudot

filipacchi
publishing

"What is essential to French art is that it absorbs all others."
André Chastel

For centuries, Paris seems to have inhaled, absorbed and assimilated all styles…. Anyone who loves to stroll around Paris, crisscrossing the streets of the capitol (particularly those with an interest in decorating), would be fascinated to know what is happening behind the city's elegant facades. Only a team from an eminent publication like *Elle Decor* could gain access to these inner sanctums and be permitted to photograph them in stunning detail. In covering everything from family dwellings to lofts, *Elle Decor* has established a rare documentation on the manner in which Parisians actually live—from the Left Bank to the Right, from neighborhood to neighborhood.

We have mixed private residences with restaurants, hotels, as well as the shops and boutiques that actually provide the beautiful wares on view in these pages. Although we do not pretend to offer exhaustive coverage, we have collected here a wonderful selection of our favorite areas of Paris. After years of research and discovery, we are happy to include the secret, never-before-published places that capture the imagination and awaken the senses.

We were privileged to be given an insider's view of these places. Remaining true to the *Elle Decor* style, this compilation demonstrates that there is more to the art of living than just the exterior trappings of wealth and luxury—a certain style, found here, under the Parisian skies.

J. D. - F. B.

CONTENTS

INTRODUCTION

Ah, to live in Paris! Only a Parisian could down play her mythological status in the eyes of the world, yet an amazing variety of people share the honor of residing behind the city's elegant walls. In Insider's Paris by Elle Decor, we have divided this diverse city into four major sections. The first section, From Saint-Germain-des-Prés to Montparnasse, covers the entire Left Bank, with its ancient buildings and artist's studios. The second section, From the Marais to the Madeleine, reveals the secret places from the Madeleine to what was once the ancient prison of the Bastille, destroyed so long ago. The third section, From Montmartre to the Beaux Quartiers, includes some of Paris's most exclusive neighborhoods, where the entrenched bourgeoisie lives alongside the artists who resurrected the legendary neighborhood of Montmartre. In our last section we find ourselves on the fringe of the city where the Marché-au-Puces and the suburbs draw city dwellers to their outer limits. Subdividing the city into four sections has simplified matters; and, as they say, to divide is to conquer! Parisians love to classify and analyze, and each individual district, a village unto itself, carries its own subtle references and social connotations. But rather than each of Paris's arrondissements—which start at the center at Ile de la Cité and spiral outward toward the suburbs—having its own unique style, we have found the opposite to be true; many things have changed in Paris over the last twenty years, and within each arrondissement we find some element of the diversity that characterizes the Paris of today.

It is interesting to note, however, that with all the social changes that have swept over Paris, people living side-by-side in neighboring districts continue to identify strongly with their own neighborhood. Each arrondissement generates an ambiance all its own: All good Parisians know, for example, that those living in the Palais-Royal area do not live by the same morays as those living near the Quai Voltaire, though they face each other across the Seine every day. Similarly, those living in Montparnasse will admit to knowing little if anything about the people in the Plaine Monceau right next door. This is also true for the faubourg Saint-Antoine neighborhood too, where they seem to deny that their neighbors to the west in the faubourg Saint-Honoré practically live on the same street. Everyone in Paris is a fan of her own parish. But in the end, the people who live within the city "walls" are, if somewhat reluctantly, supportive of each other, connected as they are by a deep, abiding—and mutual—love for their city. Though built on just a few acres, the entire world fixes its gaze on Paris's splendors. Neither war, nor short-sighted architects, city planners with political ambitions, modernity or even the global economy has been able to alter Paris's essential spirit. Its private homes, if not national treasures, often display distinctive, and distinguished features worthy of attention. Although this book gives only a small taste of the feast that is Paris, it nevertheless offers views rarely seen by those "outsiders" that make up most of the world's population. We offer here our modest contribution to revealing some of her hidden charms—a labor of love that surely lends support to the old French adage, "Paris is worth any sacrifice."

Sometimes it seems like everything has already been said about Paris. We have already been shown all of its beauty and have been apprised of its faults—one as numerous as the other: from the Eiffel Tower to the Jussieu skyscraper, the Butte aux Cailles to the hillside of Montmartre. Despite its infinite attractions, Paris is still, in reality, only a small city easy to cross on foot. From the immigrant section of la Goutte-d'Or to the faubourg Saint-Germain; from the Pont-du-Jour to Bercy; from the arch at Place du Carrousel to the Arc du Triomphe at l'Etoile—even if you happen to get lost in Paris, you can never really be "lost," because it is always easy to speak with Parisians. (It is especially easy for foreigners, as Parisians prefer to speak with them than to their own fellow citizens.) During the 20th century, only Paris has been as adept as New York City in welcoming, housing and in integrating such a variety of races and cultures. Perhaps the preamble to the French Constitution, "The Rights of Man…," does stand for something after all. Parisians speak every language but English, which seems to be relegated to coursework in school. Home to a wide variety of ethnic groups, all religions are practiced and every kind of lifestyle is available in Paris. And with its historical and cultural sites, its architecture and gorgeous settings, sightseers on both sides of the Seine are treated to a visual feast. Whether you're reading a long or a condensed version of the last 2,000 years of Paris history, so many people have written, sung about or critiqued Paris that many of them have, over time, been lost or omitted from successive texts. To give you an idea of how many there have been, the marvelous writer Jean Favier, of l'Institut de France, in his brilliant *Paris* (Fayard, 2001) has compiled in 1,008 pages an "incomplete" collection of these often passionate, almost forgotten narratives. No one who is interested in our capital will be left indifferent by it. About those who are eventually forgotten by history, Apollinaire wrote in 1918, the year of his premature death: "Men never leave things behind without some regret, even the places, things and people that made them the most unhappy; they do not let them go without feeling pain."

Indeed, the very fabric of Paris is made up of regrets that refuse to die, of dear ones who have departed, of masterpieces in constant danger, and of a collection of silent grievances. And yet the city as a whole, with all its terror and beauty, has learned how to transform itself over the years without renouncing what it essentially is—Paris has understood how to be middle class without being boring. We Parisians live rather well, and if we appear to protect ourselves a little too much from those distant "barbarians" from beyond the beltway, it's because our personal secrets are our surest guarantee for maintaining our individuality. How many invaluable masterpieces (a little Corot here, a portrait of Queen Marie-Antoinette there), still hang in some old, now-decrepit salon, where a doddering old coachman still guards the gates where carriages used to enter? How many potential museums exist at the end of some dank alleyway? What kinds of eccentricities must still exist behind those massive facades designed by Eugene Haussmann for the upper crust? Paris, initially built on a limited piece of terrain, has not only expanded physically, but has evolved socially as well. What caused Paris's social stratification, where each floor of a building, as Zola so aptly criticized in *Pot-Bouille,* was reserved for a particular social class; where the rich only crossed the poorer classes in the stairwell on their way to their attic rooms? Over the last 50 years, things have greatly changed. Those with more moderate incomes have been pushed out to the suburbs; the number of singles continues to rise, as does the average

age of the population in general. The perpetual bustle of the city, fashion and peoples' passions…all these are fuel for an engine that never stops pulsing with the rhythm of the times. Today, Paris is still the most desirable city in the world to live in, and is the best suited to represent the "heart" of Europe.

Another legendary aspect of Paris is the Parisian woman—a species that still stands out from the rest. Their particular kind of seduction is so well known that it needs no further comment. As for the Parisian male, he embodies all of the characteristics that people commonly associate with him without mentioning them aloud—the suavity and style that make him a Parisian male. Then there are those Parisians who are actually from Paris—there aren't that many, so they tend to brag about it. And then there's everyone else—all those who have come from the four corners of the planet to live here. These new Parisians consistently reinforce our distinctive identity, our wealth and our differences. Out of this melting pot, they have created wonders. But you are either from Paris or you're not, and you will never be. Just accept it; those who were there before you have decreed it so.

And then of course all these fine people need lodgings. Finding a place to live in Paris is no picnic. Many Parisians live and die in the same area, perhaps even in the same house. They have spent their entire lives looking out at their city without ever noticing themselves aging. Those who have found a place they like rarely move. In the really nice houses there are always "more behinds than chairs" as the saying goes. In Paris, we give each other the once-over. We criticize one another. The rites we observe are so subtle and arcane that even the most perceptive ethnologists become discouraged. Who among them, what Maeterlinck in their midst, will write about the Parisian ants, and describe their nests, their riches and their secret retreats? *Elle Decor* is happy for the opportunity just to photograph them, as though photographing the chimney smoke curling upward from the city that pilgrims coming from afar used to love to observe. Curiosity, it is said, killed the cat. But that has been our photographers' objective—to satisfy our insatiable curiosity about a legendary place. And these Thebans are not only full of energy; they're also full of ideas.

From African art to art deco, from Madame de Pompadour to the designer Madeleine Castaing, from bohemian chic to cosmopolitan sophistication…by simply strolling along the banks of the Seine, one can find curiosities of all kinds, collections of all kinds and a greater variety of treasures than one could ever hope to find in shops or bazaars anywhere else in the world: Kilim rugs, coral, crystals, silver, tapestries, religious icons…. African art, modern art, Gothic sculptures of Christ, Japanese stamps, antique treasures from every era and the recent resurgence of "modern" items from the 1960s…all this bric-à-brac, luxuries and objects one only dreams of, can be found in the windows and galleries of these labyrinthine streets that our reporters have tirelessly covered. Taking special care when exploring sites that have no equal, they have summoned the ancient god Asmodée to lift the roofs off these dwellings so we can observe, acquaint ourselves and finally understand what transpires inside these Parisian homes. For this book we set out in search of Parisians who live well—in true Parisian style—no matter what their circumstances. *Insider's Paris* is an homage to diversity, to people's fantasies and to their creative free will that, surprisingly, often manifests itself in the form of simple common sense. Even with all the diverse inclinations and never-ending alterations, a certain unity emerges. Perhaps it is what people refer to as "the spirit of Paris."

Under the Mirabeau Bridge there flows the Seine
Must I recall
Our loves recall how then
After each sorrow joy came back again
Let night come on bells end the day
The days go by me still I stay.

("*The Mirabeau Bridge*" Guillaume Apollinaire, trans. Richard Wilbur, Random House)

Paris wasn't born yesterday; it has 2,000 years of history behind it. It has experienced wave after wave of immigrants and has evolved slowly from the time of the Gallo-Romans, culminating with the authoritarian urbanization of the city under Napoleon III by the civil engineer Eugene Haussmann. Despite the ruthless destruction that has taken place in modern-day Paris, the basic layout of the streets and the initial shape of the city has not changed a bit. This is perhaps the secret to its uniqueness and to its enduring charm. Its urbanization is based on its history, beginning with the Hôtel de Ville (Paris's City Hall) to Place de la Concorde. From there, it continues in a straight line from the Champs-Elysées to the modern complex of buildings known as la Défense; on out to the terraces of Saint-Germain-en-Laye. The Seine, in contrast, gradually meanders away from this straight line, with the city's greatest monuments embellishing both sides of its banks: the Université de Paris, the Palais des Beaux-Arts, the Grand Louvre, the Hôtel des Invalides, the Ecole Militaire and the Palais de Chaillot. Symmetrically aligned are the Assemblée Nationale and the church of the Madeleine.

The walls that once demarcated the periphery of this magnificent city (which was then only a fortified village) were built and rebuilt over the ages, each time farther away from its center. Today there is almost nothing left of that original wall built around the city in 1190 by King Philippe Auguste. By the 19th century, the working-class areas expanded out to the exterior boulevards, which had been built over the top of the city's ancient fortifications. From that point outward, there is "la zone" where a mixture of people live. The outlying beltway, constructed under de Gaulle's presidency in the 1960s, came to represent by its circle of concrete just where the city limits were. From that point on, the city could grow only via its suburbs. The metro system, built in 1900, did not go out that far. (Originally the fortifications around Paris had doors that could be closed when necessary to keep intruders out. Today, these doors exist in name only.) Paris institutions have all developed within parameters that have not changed since the 19th century. Beyond the beltway, we find a bustling world—the working-class residential areas—in other words, the suburbs. Paris either controls things or it resists them, for in Paris all business activities are centrally operated.

Within such a geographically restricted area, greenery is a luxury, a lawn is an event and private gardens are a rarity. Paris is populated by people who dream of wide-open spaces. The luckier ones will move out toward the western part of the city, where the land, being less populated, gives them the illusion of living in the country. At the beginning of the 20th century, far from the foul-smelling smoke that belched forth from indus-

industries developing in the eastern part of the city, the wealthier denizens got to breathe the clean air of the Bois de Boulogne. Another kind of segregation, that began at the beginning of the 20th century, came about by the invention of the elevator. Whether a building had an elevator or not came to affect its real-estate value. After the easily accessible first floor, comes all the other floors which are less so. As time passed, buildings were built higher and with more floors. During the 19th century, the city got running water and gas heat…but the maids still had to climb to their rooms under the eaves on the very top floors. In 1954, garbage chutes suddenly appeared, but by then it didn't really matter what floor you lived on; what mattered was whether you lived in the city or not. Transportation problems still existed, though, and if anything, with the snarl of traffic and metro strikes, got worse. In the past, when there was no public transportation, people in the suburbs had to leave their homes early, sometimes in the middle of the night to get to their jobs in the city on foot. This shadowy mass that we call the working class often found themselves mingling with crowds of late-night revelers.

Today, this metropolis called Paris is almost a whole new city. Around 1900, at the time of the famous doorman at the exclusive nightclub Chez Maxim's, the 200,000 or so Parisians were on familiar terms with one another, frequented the same clubs, flirted with the same beautiful women, died side-by-side in the heroic battles of world wars and ended up in the Père-Lachaise cemetery. That Paris no longer exists, although the "upper crust" (which is as ancient as the Jurassic age) which has always existed, still lives on today, followed by the "nouveaux riches," who came from all over the world. Today, they have evolved into that category of people who are old and venerable and though often poor are generally well housed. During the 1920s, 1950s and 1980s, an infusion of the young flocked to Paris and upset the established order of things. In the '20s, Cubism started influencing the world of decorating; in the '50s, there was a craving for all the modern products that the Americans were touting. In the '80s, a "politically correct" culture appeared whose byword, paradoxically, was "caviar." And although Louis XVI himself was guillotined, his style proved impossible to dethrone. The French, it appears, always seem to return to the neoclassic.

Now, silk-screen prints by Andy Warhol and works by avant-garde artists available only to the rich lend a little craziness to the most conservative homes. "I'm not just another pretty face," Marilyn seems to say from where she hangs on an 18th-century paneled wall. Sculptures by César, Niki de Saint-Phalle and Fontana blend well in ancient townhouses. Here we find a chest of drawers by Boulle; idols from the Cyclade islands and easy chairs by Mies Van der Rohe. Since WW II, eclecticism has ruled—a mixture of decorating styles, ancient and modern. To add to the mix, the flea market and the Surrealists joined forces to, in their words, "cross umbrellas with sewing machines on multiple dissecting tables." First came the invasion of Majorelle's art nouveau furniture and Gallé's creations in glass, then came those art deco divans set at right angles. With the 1960s came the advent of "design" with all its new expressions and ways of marketing. All followed by the arrival of housing for people of moderate incomes: "something nice for everyone," as they said. Unfortunately, this resulted in no one having anything unusual. The '70s brought "retro"-—from laquerware by Ruhlmann to calendars of Vargas pin-ups, the film *Victor-Victoria*, Borsalino and Company, boas worn by Régine and fake Chapirus. The reissuing of Mallet and Stevens's 1934 book on modern architecture (along with silk-screens designed and conceived of by young artists) resulted in a new style for a new age—a style that harmonized well with American loft-style living. The kitchen became a bar. The bed was king-size. The bathroom opened out onto the living quarters, like you might find in an emergency ward. While Mozart's music was still a mainstay, art deco works by Reynaud were considered contemporary. As for the last part of the century, it seemed to detach itself from its earlier emotions to go way back to things nearly forgotten altogether: chandeliers, ornamental screens and canopied beds all made a comeback, as did the word "charm." But contemporary art was still without question paramount. This was especially true in photography, an art easily accessible to everyone. The new styles were influenced by and mixed in with the styles of the 18th century. The 20th century began and ended under the influence of the neo-Louis XVI style of decoration, first made popular by the writers Helleu, Proust and the brothers Goncourt. But by the end of the century, it was stripped of its lavishness. With the new millennium came the second death of Marie-Antoinette. Once again, lavish apartments were emptied of their treasures, but this time by American millionaires. Today, we no longer clamor for their return. Instead, we borrow the American style—like their raw-brick walls, for example, that goes so well with sketches by Cy Twombly.

And while we fuss around trying to decide whether to hire an upholsterer or an interior decorator, whether we prefer practical women or women of the world, men of taste or—but what taste are we talking about? The Seine river continues to flow beneath the bridges of Paris. It crosses the capital in the shape of a crescent moon. The length of its arc extends seven and a half miles from Boulogne in the west to Bercy in the east. Thirty-nine bridges and footbridges link the opposite banks (and their often-antagonistic residents). And even though one doesn't have to be a bohemian agitator to live on the Left Bank, the myth, the legend no doubt contributes to ones sense of being there. And at great expense, mind you, as the price one now pays per square foot of living space in the Saint-Germain-des-Prés area is greater than just about anywhere else in Paris. As for living on the Right Bank...no one brags about it, but it is not completely void of originality. The very exclusive apartments of the 16th arrondissement that were detested only yesterday, have been rediscovered by the trendy bourgeoisie who now live there, unless they've decided instead to move to the fashionable lofts of the Saint-Antoine neighborhood. Open space has become synonymous with reclaiming a kind of freedom.

Although Paris's "melting pot" is limited to some degree by its external boundaries and by the forests that encircle it, it has nevertheless been able, despite its small size, to redefine its social topography through its geography. People with diverse lifestyles observe each other and oppose each other in order to, in the end, understand one another. Paris remains a city of contrasts, with its luxuries, its office buildings; its well-fed citizens and its homeless; its shopping malls and health food stores, traffic jams and public works. It's a city of deep hurts and fleeting moments of happiness. Parisians scurry about on this square patch of land with all their contradictions, their conformity and their quirkiness. They love to be at home, but at the drop of a hat they can be found marching in solidarity with strikers in the streets. They have read everything, seen everything and have done just about everything. And at the end of the day, they know that Paris is the worst place to live—except for anywhere else.

François Baudot

from SAINT-GERMAIN DES-PRĒS *to* MONTPARNASSE

The Left Bank, as we say in Paris, is above all a state of mind. In the Paris of old there were those who wouldn't dream of crossing the Seine to visit the Right Bank. Parisians, of course, often choose to live on the Right Bank, yet consider the cafés, bookstores and the houses of Saint-Germain-des-Prés their territory as well. In the 1970s, when the famous designer Yves Saint Laurent decided to open his first boutique carrying his ready-to-wear collection in rue de Tournon, he named it "Rive Gauche" (Left Bank). The connotation was clear—there was no better way to express the panache and style that came to define the legendary Left Bank.

The Right Bank, in contrast, is a vast business sector, refuge to the upper-middle classes and the lumpen proletariat. The Left Bank, home to the aristocracy, was also claimed by those other patricians revered and canonized in the great Parisian tradition: philosophers, anarchists, artists, loafers and foreigners in love with the Paris mystique. But the intellectuals of the old Left Bank have increasingly given way to a new bourgeoisie and the rooms and cafés that harbored agitators of the avant-garde, now sport boutiques with all manner of luxury items.

Today, a strong sense of an elegant kind of "neglected comfort" has replaced the rooms of old where people sought to change the world. The isolationist stance of the Left Bank has not stopped an invasion from the Right Bank. The 1980s saw the arrival of jewelry and clothing stores and those high-end accessories usually associated with the most exclusive neighborhoods and luxury hotels. Some retailers, longing for a certain cultural (to say nothing of artistic) legitimacy migrated to the Left Bank for its instant caché. This trend signaled the evolution of a fashion where authenticity became a byword for success. When a well-known trade name installed itself in Saint-Germain-des-Prés, it signalled a distancing from the world of flashy consumerism to align itself with things that endure. The historical buildings, bookstores for intellectuals and bibliophiles, the legendary cafés all represent the spirit of the Left Bank. Now, as a sign of the times, one

Left
The Eglise Saint-Germain.

Next spread
1. The cloister at the Ecole des Beaux-Arts.
2. The Palais du Sénat.
3. The café Les Deux Magots.
4. Quai Voltaire, the building's courtyard is hidden behind a carriage entranceway.
5. The four seasons fountain.
6. L'Institut de France seen from the garden.
7. The Panthéon.
8. The famous brasserie La Closerie des Lilas, behind the statue of Maréchal Ney.

from SAINT-GERMAIN-DES-PRĒS

frequently sees books being used as props in luxury stores; but not just any books—books by such authors as Lacan, Cioran and Duras, who haunted the Left Bank in days gone by and now serve as indicators of the standards of numerous establishments all madly in search of times past.

Another sign of the times is the renewed interest in the 19th-century passion for natural history and taxidermy; for shells, stuffed creatures, curios and scientific objects. This mixture of things that evince a curiosity about the natural world and the life of the mind, like a jumble of items displayed in a mirrored curio cabinet, seem to reflect back to Parisians their own changing image.

What still remains, and will always endure are the ancient houses and garrets that despite their being increasingly taken over by the boutiques of the boulevard Saint-Germain, still maintain their integrity and charm—some dating back to the 17th and 18th centuries. Their influence on newer buildings is evident; they have inspired both the design and the layout of newer apartments in their emphasis on light, and more importantly, in their preoccupation with plants and gardens in their design—an element found only in this section of Paris. These are some of the factors that have contributed to the 6th arrondissement's growing status over the last few years as the most expensive place in the city to live. Many fashionable foreigners want to have a pied-à-terre here—add to this already cosmopolitan atmosphere French nobles and elderly dowagers dressed in black, all living side-by-side with moneyed sophisticates and you get a good idea of the eclectic and interesting mix that is Saint-Germain-des-Prés.

While business lunches are all the rage across Paris, in the Saint-Germain-des-Prés to Montparnasse area they have reached a pinnacle; literary feasts, celebrations of the spirit, the "commerce" of ideas. In the famous cafés like Les Deux Magots, Café de Flore and Brasserie Lipp, this genre of lunches have flourished more than in the larger cafés of Montparnasse, despite the growth of tourism. In the 1920s, Montparnasse cafés were the preferred haunts of the artists and writers who frequented them. Although café society disappeared long ago, the legends live on—legends like the one of Saint-Michel. On the strength of its reputation alone, it has been embraced by young suburbanites looking for a remedy for the relative quiet (and relative boredom) of suburban life. Unfortunately, the boutiques that followed suburban shoppers to the Left Bank displaced those that had until then carried wares that exhibited an original

to MONTPARNASSE

mixture of cultures and tastes. Up until 1968, eclectic shops existed side-by-side like nowhere else in Paris. The famous student revolts in that year left their mark on Paris's Left Bank. Whether it was an elitist or a populist revolution back then, the repercussions of that period are still being felt today. Fortunately, as the famous singer Charles Trenet sang, "Long, long after the poets have disappeared, their songs still linger in the streets."

Those who live in Montparnasse have a bit of the artist in them and their lodgings reflect that element. We see more sky and more trees there, and the Place Denfert-Rochereau has more of a feeling of the countryside about it than anywhere in Paris. Hidden among more modern buildings are villas, villages and marketplaces hidden to outsiders who are unaware of the life behind. So the inhabitants, if they prefer, can remain insulated from the outside world.

Another bastion of the Left Bank, isolated from the main boulevard is the sacred (and arduously steep) Montagne Sainte-Geneviève. First, you cross the boulevard Saint-Michel taking care to avoid some very ugly thoroughfares lined with what appear to be modest homes with sandstone facades. Upon reaching the summit, in the shadow of the Panthéon, one discovers ancient back streets with houses and porches so old that they might well have sheltered the Three Musketeers, heard the poems of Verlaine or the convent school pupils reciting their Latin declensions.

Montmartre's more famous Place du Tertre is the Right Bank equivalent to Montagne Sainte-Geneviève with its Place de la Contrescarpe. Over the years, it too has been flooded with sightseeing buses, but this should not deter a stroll along the hillside—as one does in Montmartre—with the same feeling of being someplace far away. And indeed, when these two places are mentioned people say, "It's so far away," even though they have no real cause to say so. For nothing in the capital, no matter how far from the center of Paris (about where the Pyramid stands in the courtyard of the Louvre), is farther than three miles away. Even today Paris, and the Left Bank in particular, remains a city best experienced on foot.

A COLLECTOR'S ELEGANT ABODE

Opposite page:
François-Joseph Graf
designed the library,
dining room and den in
this townhouse in the
7th arrondissement.
In one room, a rich
celadon green enobles
the walls; in the other,
red flannel serves as the
backdrop for a series of
early 19th-century
botanical engravings.
The armchairs are made
of ebony and gilded
bronze (Westenholz,
England, 19th century).
Above: An alcove in
the library with a
series of 18th-century
English engravings
by Thomas Frye.

An 18th-century English mahogany bureau stands between two French windows in a living room on Faubourg Saint-Germain which overlooks the garden. The comfortable sofa and armchairs are by Decourt. Sage green walls bring out the tones of a striking late 17th-century painting by St. John Baptiste Medina. The curtain fabric is from Fortuny in Venice. Room designed by François-Joseph Graf.

Right: In this living room-library, the woodwork is in the Louis XVI style and the parquet is in the "Versailles" style. The library's English mahogany stepladder is from the 18th century (Westenholz). A 17th-century Turkish rug from Oushak lends the room vibrancy.
Below: A painting by Brazilian artist Reynaldo Fonseca.

STROLLING THROUGH SAINT-GERMAIN-DES-PRĒS

1. LES MARRONNIERS *A small, shaded courtyard adjacent to what was once Delacroix's studio; one of the area's most lovely and best kept secrets.*
21, rue Jacob, 75006.
Phone: +33 1 43 25 30 60.

2. LA MAISON DE BRUNE *Lamps in bronze patina, heavy oak furniture, a drawing, woven cloth with a color scheme of dark brown, green and plum.*
23, rue du Cherche-Midi, 75006.
Phone: +33 1 42 22 98 86.

3. GALERIE DENIS DORIA
This merchant's austerity and preference for rationalist architecture has made him one of the foremost specialists on modern art.
16, rue de Seine, 75006.
Phone: +33 1 43 25 43 25.

4. HUILERIE LEBLANC *This small boutique carries an extensive variety of pure oils, from olive oil to pine cone oil.*
6, rue Jacob, 75006.
Phone: +33 1 46 34 61 55.

5. ROYAL ARROW
Benches, lounge chairs, plant tubs... all made of teak, the outdoor material par excellence.
206, boulevard Saint-Germain, 75006.
Phone: +33 1 45 49 49 89.

6. LIBRAIRIE MARITIME ET D'OUTRE-MER
There's an air of the high seas blowing through this publishing house and bookstore, where model sailboats, maps and books are all "seaworthy."
17, rue Jacob, 75006.
Phone: +33 1 46 33 47 48.

7. MUSÉE MAILLOL *A beautiful museum founded by Dina Vierny, the master's model and heir, with her own funds.*
Along with the permanent collection, the museum hosts changing exhibitions.
61, rue de Grenelle, 75007.
Phone: +33 1 42 22 59 58.

8. GALERIE CATHERINE MEMMI
The lines of the house, the furniture and accessories, all adhere to the same rigorous simplicity.
11, rue Saint-Sulpice, 75006.
Phone: +33 1 44 07 02 02.

9. DEBAUVE ET GALLAIS *The setting here is magnificent—a palace for discerning palates. A chocolate store that has satisfied sweet-toothes from the time of the First Empire.*
30, rue des Saints-Pères, 75007.
Phone: +33 1 45 48 54 67

10. LA CASA DEL HABANO
A Cuban enclave just steps away from the Brasserie Lipp. Here one can buy any hard-to-find cigars.
169, boulevard Saint-Germain, 75006.
Phone: +33 1 45 49 24 30

11. MAISON DE FAMILLE *Assembled here are all those practical things we'd like to have in our own homes; linens, kitchen accessories, furniture, both sensible and charming.*
29, rue Saint-Sulpice, 75006.
Phone: +33 1 40 46 97 47.

12. FRAGONARD *A gift shop for every occasion, from fragrant things to bric-à-brac...tasteful temptations for the epicure.*
196, boulevard Saint-Germain, 75007.
Phone: +33 1 42 84 12 12

13. ARCADE OF RUE DE VAUGIRARD
A sheltered arcade where one can stroll alongside the Luxembourg, the Left Bank's largest garden, between the rue de Rennes and de l'Odéon.

1

2

3

4

5 6

7 8

9 10

11

12 13

Right page and below:
Beneath the blue skies of Saint-Germain, on the corner of rue Jacob and rue Bonaparte, lies the famous Ladurée. Who would ever guess, with its old-fashioned facade and traditional delicacies, that it was actually built in this century?

RUE BONAPARTE
DELICACIES FOR EVERY SENSE

Right: This was once the office and boutique of Madeleine Castaing — one of the greatest interior decorators and antiques dealers of the postwar era. With such elegant delicacies the pastry chef has sought to recapture the Balzacian atmosphere that Castaing so loved. Interior decorator Roxane Rodriguez created this delightful ambiance.

Between the first and second floors of the old houses that lead to the Seine, mezzanines, with their low ceilings, make cozy intimate cocoons where the romanticism affiliated with richly upholstered furniture from the 19th century sets the mood—as seen here on the second floor of the Ladurée tea salon. This exquisite room, with sumptuous fabrics and late 19th-century photographs, transports guests to another era.

STRENGTH AND SIMPLICITY

Designer and interior
decorator Catherine
Memmi lives here amid
her own creations, and
practices the same
austere sense of luxury
at home that is found in
her boutiques. The long
sofa is covered in
pristine white linen,
on the low Wenge-wood
table a ceramic dish
tastefully displays
unusually colored
candles. Between the
two windows is a
painting by
Hilton McConnico.

This office also serves
as a dining room.
Catherine Memmi
designed the wood table
and the bookcase in
bleached ash, where
multicolored ceramics
are exhibited along with
files and boxes created
by Marie Papier.
The chairs are covered
in Memmi's signature
natural linen and the
cotton curtains are
backed in percale.
Unique adjustable
floor lamps are by
Christophe Delcourt.

THE UNUSUAL REIGNS

An Italian client who
loves the unusual
entrusted the interior
design of her pied-à-
terre on a second floor
of this townhouse on
rue de Verneuil to
Stéphanie Cauchoix.
The woodwork is painted
in a pale gray wash.
The life-size horse is
made of papier
mâché—a 19th-century
saddler's prop to
advertise harnesses
(Actéon collection).
A startling mannequin
with adjustable limbs sits
on the couch (Cauchoix).
In the foreground,
a Napoleon-era camp
bed is covered in linen.
A 17th-century
Venetian mirror hangs
unexpectedly over
a wall mirror
(Galerie Meyer).

In Saint-Germain,
a certain bourgeois
bohemia allows for an
array of styles—classic
and modern, minimal
and ornate all
harmonize in the mix.
Here, ancient furniture
goes well with the more
industrial-style railway
racks from the 1950s
used here as bookcases.
An 18th-century day
bed is upholstered
with an Indian quilt.
The eclecticism exhibited
here produces a kind
of fantasy world,
awash in the light
streaming in through
the high windows.

STROLLING THROUGH SAINT-GERMAIN-DES-PRĒS

1. LE SAINT-GRÉGOIRE *Cozy, elegant and not too big, this refuge has more than earned its reputation as a "hotel of charm."*
43, rue de l'Abbé Grégoire, 75006.
Phone: +33 1 45 48 23 23.

2. FARROW AND BALL *Enough colors to satisfy any and all tastes and wallpaper available in the most refined tones: the caviar of housepaints.*
50, rue de l'Université, 75007.
Phone: +33 1 45 44 47 94.

3. LE JOUR ET L'HEURE *A little piece of England; stationery, pens, famous Smythson notebooks from Bond Street, soap, plaid throws and small but exquisite leather goods.*
6, rue du Dragon, 75006.
Phone: +33 1 42 22 96 11.

4. À SAINT-BENOÎT-DES-PRÉS
A mini-bookstore with a remarkable, eclectic selection of books and posters.
2, rue Saint-Benoît, 75006.
Phone: +33 1 40 20 43 42.

5. CABINET DE CURIOSITÉS
A paradise of the unexpected; here rare and puzzling objects converge. A little of everything, but not just anything.
23, rue de Beaune, 75007.
Phone: +33 1 42 61 09 57.

6. LA PALETTE *An institution suspended in time. A rough but friendly reception, inexpensive red wines and cured meats delight tourists and regulars alike.*
43, rue de Seine, 75006.
Phone: +33 1 43 26 68 15.

7. LE CACHEMIRIEN *The great woven fabrics of India, from Pashmina to Benares brocades—a boutique that specializes in items that keep the cold at bay.*
13, rue de Tournon, 75006.
Phone: +33 1 43 29 93 82.

8. MOISSONNIER *Builders of fine furniture since 1885. A repertoire of objects with finely detailed features exquisitely rendered inspired by the 18th-century style.*
28, rue du Bac, 75007.
Phone: +33 1 42 61 84 88.

9. DAUM *A prestigious name since the early 20th century, the Left Bank branch of this store, which specializes in crystal and sintered glass, also carries work by such luminaries as Philippe Starck and Hilton McConnico.*
167, boulevard Saint-Germain, 75006.
Phone: +33 1 42 22 16 12.

10. LA DUCHESSE BRISÉE *A team of young virtuosos runs this tapestry and upholstery store: drapes, upholstery fabrics, curtains, ornamental accessories...all that is beautiful.*
14, rue des Saints-Pères, 75006.
Phone: +33 1 53 33 83 83.

11. RUE MONSIEUR-LE-PRINCE
An exquisite 18th-century door.

12. HERVÉ LORGERÉ *This relatively small space—in relation to the clutter of objects—only serves to accentuate the air of discovery in this paradise of the unexpected.*
25, rue des Saints-Pères, 75006.
Phone: +33 1 42 86 02 02.

4   5

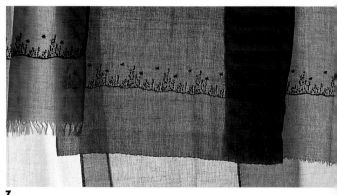

7

9   10

2 3

6

8

11 12

41

NEOCLASSICISM IN CLOSE QUARTERS

In the antiques dealer
Alexandre Biaggi's
library, situated over
his store, we find his
books, catalogues and
drawings from every
era arranged snugly;
the sculptures are from
the late 19th century.
The Charles X desk
of blond wood goes
perfectly with a 1930s
armchair. The side table
is by Jacques Adnet.

43

All the charm of this cozy dining room overlooking the rue de Seine emanates from the rapport between its small size, the delicate lines of the furniture (in the Directoire style), and the colossal bust of Minerva (Biaggi collection). The antique silverware is by Christofle, the cut-crystal candleholders are from the 19th century and the plates are by Christian Lacroix for Christofle.

AN EXERCISE IN STYLE

Yves Gastou took a gamble when he introduced 1940s and '50s furniture in this elegant 18th-century townhouse owned by a Parisian collector. In the foreground a casual pair of oak stools are offset by a bronze armchair with a leather seat (André Arbus, 1952) and a coffee table made by the iron craftsman Gilbert Poillerat, all resting on a rug by Arbus. The vases are Venetian glass.

THE COUNTRYSIDE IN PARIS

This duplex has
a double theme:
flowers and music
(jasmine, lavender,
mimosa, traditional
roses…and the cello).
The arched bay
window in the bedroom
opens onto a garden
terrace encircled
by a zinc flower box.
The teak lounge
chair is resistant
to Parisian rain.

Left: The bathroom is both simple and refined, with its traditional linens and reassembled doors dating back to the 19th century. *Above:* In the large studio-music room, light filters through a skylight of frosted glass. The wide oak-plank floors were specially made in the Aveyron region of France. A pair of Renaissance-style lead flower basins grace on either side of the steps. The elegant Bechstein piano and the cello belong to the master of the house.

RUE
DES BEAUX-ARTS
L'HŌTEL

This beautiful hotel,
situated on rue des
Beaux-Arts, needs no
other name than L'Hôtel.
It became famous when
Oscar Wilde, then exiled
in Paris, died there in
abject poverty — very
incongruous indeed to
the sumptuous Empire-
style dining room that
characterizes the hotel
today. L'Hôtel was
recently restored
by Jacques Garcia.

A LARGE COLLECTION IN A LIMITED SPACE

Interior decorator
Jacques Leguennec's
library reflects his wide
variety of literary
interests — each section
is arranged by subject
matter. The inviting
sofas (Schwartz) are
covered in raw linen
(Lauer). In front of the
window a lecture stand
made of white-painted
oak holds the interesting
book of the moment
(studio Leguennec).
A Picasso drawing
lends sophistication;
the unique sculptural
lamp behind the sofa
is by Alain Ozanne.

Ozanne and Leguennec both have a fondness for collecting and have devised ways to show their collections to their best advantage in a small space. Paintings, curios in wood, autographs and a variety of delightful objects are cleverly arranged on buttress-shelves, thereby avoiding the sometimes tedious symmetry of hanging things. The mantle becomes a display shelf where a 19th-century articulated mannequin holds court above a trompe-l'oeil drawing by Pascale Laurent.

RUE DE L'ÉCHAUDÉ
A FLAIR FOR FASHION AND PHOTOGRAPHY

When Karl Lagerfeld and this old notions shop *(above)* met up, it was immediate synergy. Lagerfeld installed his personal office here, facing a gallery converted by Andrée Putman that houses a variety of perfumes, clothing and photographs signed by the artist. In the front of the space a staircase is cleverly concealed; a custom display table *(right)*, and wash basin *(left)* were both designed by Andrée Putman.

1

STROLLING THROUGH
SAINT-GERMAIN-DES-PRĒS

1. BRASSERIE LIPP
The smart set and followers all show up here, not so much for the quality of the comestibles as for the interesting clientele. The 1900 decor is a historical landmark.
151, boulevard Saint-Germain, 75006.
Phone: +33 1 45 48 53 91.

2. ATELIER MARC DEKEISTER *He loves Dürer, Vermeer and…comics. Strongly influenced by all, his portrait paintings of houses are of the highest quality.*
32, rue Saint-Guillaume, 75007.
Phone: +33 1 45 44 99 75

3. MADELEINE GÉLY *This highly respected vendor won't sell you an umbrella, but she'll honor you by allowing you to buy one!*
218, boulevard Saint-Germain, 75007.
Phone: +33 1 42 22 63 35.

4. GALERIE 54 *Works by Prouvé and other designers from the 1950s occupy this austere but perfect space.*
54, rue Mazarine, 75006.
Phone: +33 1 43 26 89 96

5. UPLA *The shoulder bags that once made this name famous now rest alongside a new line of luggage and tableware in a large welcoming loft.*
5, rue Saint-Benoît, 75006.
Phone: +33 1 40 15 10 75

6. THE FOUNTAIN DE MÉDICIS
In the spring lovers rendezvous here in the shade of the Luxembourg Gardens.

7. LA GALERIE MODERNE
Once "modern," these works are now considered antiques. All those things that only yesterday were

old-fashioned are now sought after collector's pieces.
52, rue Mazarine, 75006.
Phone: +33 1 46 33 13 59.

8. CLAUDE NATURE *There isn't anyone else quite like this naturalist when it comes to locating just the right little critter. Taxidermy madness!*
6, rue des Chantiers, 75005.
Phone: +33 1 44 07 30 79.

9. TECTONA *A teak paradise—from traditional designs for English gardens, to new creations by young designers.*
36, rue du Bac, 75007.
Phone: +33 1 47 03 05 05

**10. JEAN-CLAUDE GUÉRIN
& PHILIPPE RAPIN** *We find quality antiques and the sound judgement of two dealers who are masters in the art of mixing styles.*
25, quai Voltaire, 75007.
Phone: +33 1 42 61 24 21

11. LOUIS XV FACADE *on rue de Seine. Easy to sculpt, limestone is one of the materials that characterized Paris of old.*

12. L'HÔTEL DE BRANCAS *The Institut Français d'Architecture organizes thematic exhibitions in the annex of this grand old house just next door to the Palais du Sénat.*

**13. L'ÉCOLE NATIONALE SUPÉRIEURE
DES BEAUX-ARTS**
Architecturally, each pavilion has its own style. All together, they constitute a museum of styles.
14, rue Bonaparte, 75006.
Phone: +33 1 47 03 50 00.

4   5

7

9   10

2 3

6

8

11 12 13

RUE DE L'ABBAYE-PLACE FURSTENBERG
A NAME SYNONYMOUS WITH STYLE

Right: One might think they'd walked right into someone's home, but everything here is for sale. Flamant is an unusual boutique with a certain provincial style, a touch of England, a breath of Scandinavia; the ensemble of this potpourri opens onto one of Paris's prettiest squares *(above).* Not far away is the Delacroix museum-studio with its charming little gardens.

A HARMONY OF TONES

Yves and Michèle Halard—a designer and an interior decorator—frequently change addresses, yet each of their residences gives the feeling that they've always lived there. Their passion for fabrics inspires them to mix different materials in unexpected ways. They are a study in independence, smack in the middle of the ultra-traditional neighborhood of Saint-Sulpice.

The dining room, with its purple walls and windows dressed with antique curtains, brings to mind the old-fashioned atmosphere of the ancient streets nearby. A wall light in zinc, tablecloths, plates and silverware all by Yves Halard.

RUE JACOB

LIKE SNOW IN THE SUN

Monic Fisher, Blanc d'Ivoire's designer, mixes quilts with decorative objects. She loves to juxtapose high quality with refined simplicity. Combining the classic with the exotic, the traditional with the modern, her house in Saint-Germain-des-Prés is an extension of her popular boutique *(above)*.

Next spread:
In the living room an ornamental screen made of shutters allows light to filter through from the bay window. On the low table, a taffeta quilt changes color with the light (Blanc d'Ivoire) and contrasts with a sofa covered in canvas (Frey) and a comfortable leather armchair (Flea market, 1930s).

THE CHARM OF TIME SUSPENDED

Near the Quai d'Orsay, designer Michelle Joubert includes taxidermy, for which she has a soft spot, in her eclectic decor *(see next spread)*. At the far end of the living room an 18th-century Italian banquette complements a 1950s Baguès chandelier. In the foreground on the left, a library table accommodates a candelabra by Christian Tortu. To the right, a whimsical wooden elephant (Vivement Jeudi).

Left: In a large neo-Gothic viewing case, a collection of stuffed birds contemplates an armchair in the Directoire style. *Above:* The library staircase—hold on to the banister!

DEYROLLE'S BESTIARY

For nearly two centuries, lovers of natural history ended up at Deyrolle, in one of the most beautiful townhouses on rue de Bac. Amid exotic animals and birds are shelves and drawers full of insects, fossils and shells. The site was specifically designed in the 18th century to house this comprehensive collection, and its atmosphere, though iconoclastic, is perfect for its fascinating collection.

STROLLING THROUGH QUAI VOLTAIRE

1, 2, 4 & 5. *Plaques, like the ones pictured here on the Quai Voltaire, adorn the dwellings of old Saint-Germain, helping us to imagine the district's illustrious past.*

3. *The Restaurant Voltaire, in a converted tabac, is now one of the most popular spots in this district of antiques dealers.*

6. *The Pont des Arts footbridge was one of the first examples of metal architecture in Paris. On beautiful days, many people traverse the bridge for its magnificent views. François Le Vau's masterpiece extends the axis of the chapel of the Académie Française.*

7. *The Seine, and many a love affair, flow beneath the bridges of Paris....*

8. *Created by the iron craftsman Raymond Sube at the end of the 1930s, these telescopic obelisks, situated at the four corners of the Pont du Carrousel, dramatically illuminate the night.*

9 & 10. *Two views of the prestigious Camoin gallery. Ring the bell and famous decorator Alain Demachy will invite you into his space. He juxtaposes furniture and objects from all eras, chosen with two criteria in mind: originality and quality. 9, quai Voltaire, 75007. Phone: +33 1 42 61 82 06.*

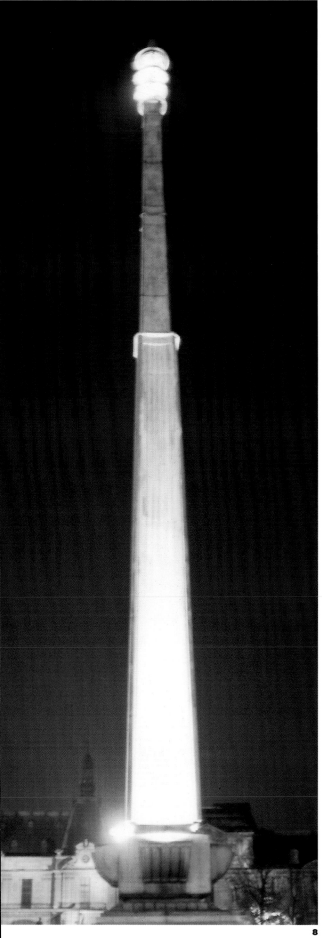

8

9

10

THE MAJESTY OF THE 18TH CENTURY REVISITED

Conjuring up the past without nostalgia; displaying beautiful old books to their greatest advantage; mixing a touch of the spirit of Provence with the elegant orderliness of the Place du Palais-Bourbon — that is what Michelle Joubert does to impart that feeling of a family manor to her interiors.
Above, left: A large bookcase with dove-gray shelves, a Dagobert armchair and a studio table of bleached walnut create a distinctive ambiance (Vivement Jeudi).
Below, left: An eclectic collection of globes.
Right page: In the dining room a mirror rests on an easel, and a carafe from the 18th century in the Spanish "Infante" style graces the table.

HIGH DRAMA AND
ECLECTICISM UNITE

Theatricality is an understatement at this basement-*cum*-gallery on boulevard Saint-Germain.

Here, each item is unique: a velvet-covered ladder for the delicate-footed. On the shelves, unusual drawings by Laurent de Comines mingle with items of unprecedented flair and imagination.

The 'ADORATION' DESIGNED BY SIR E·BVRNE·JONES

The great designer Yves Saint Laurent transformed this garden-level room into a salon-library that juxtaposes and harmonizes a variety of masterpieces from his personal collection.
Far left: A tapestry by the Pre-Raphaelite painter Edward Burne-Jones (c. 1860) hangs majestically over a table conceived by the sculptor Marcial Berro.

ART DECO OPIUM

Antique crater and torso, candlestick holders made of rock crystal, bronzes from the 17th-century, Régence seats and a rug by Da Silva Bruhns all blend magnificently.
Above, right: In front of the fireplace and its overmantel mirror (c. 1930s), rests a unique boot rack made of python by Dunand (c. 1920s). The painting is by Mondrian; the bronzes from the Fontainebleau school and the bulls are by Gianbologna.
Below, right: Beneath a large *kouros* sit portraits of Yves Saint Laurent's dog Moujik by Andy Warhol.

Top: A collection assembled by Yves Saint Laurent was given a stunning arrangement by Jacques Grange in compartments with security glass backed in velvet.

Above: On the terrace, the bird chairs are by François-Xavier Lalanne.

Right: The living room's oak bookcases painted in lead white were designed by Grange, and the chairs in apricot leather were upholstered by Decourt. To the left, a male nude by Géricault.

Just a few steps from rue Mouffetard lies the house of two antiques dealers who open their doors every Thursday to exhibit their finds to a clientele of initiates. Hence the name of their small enterprise, "Vivement Jeudi," or "I can't wait for Thursday!" *Above:* In the garden, a prolific vine, a few acacias, verbena and gooseberries. The terrace is done in brick. *Right:* In the kitchen, an artistic mix of still lifes with sweets.

A TASTE OF THE PROVINCES BEHIND THE PANTHEON

Left, clockwise from top left:
In Dominique and Pierre Bénard-Dépalle's living room the mantel serves as a landing for their various discoveries.

A Louis XVI-style table whose surface is made up of sections of stone fit together; some light furniture with openwork makes for a kind of organized disorder;

a graceful Italian chest of drawers (c. 1760); a still life of things from the sea.
Above: An oval table from the late 18th century upon which

garden implements and a notably large wooden vase with Chinese decorations, among other curiosities, provide interesting clutter.

IN THE SPIRIT OF THE 1930s

Joëlle Mortier Vallat lives in a quiet apartment that opens onto the large gardens of the Ecole des Beaux-Arts. In the inter-connecting rooms, painted in pale tones, African art and art deco live side by side with a touch of the Baroque. The large mirror is a cast from a gilded 18th-century Italian-style wooden frame. Between the two windows, a "witch's mirror" by Line Vautrin.

Here is a glimpse of antiques dealer Joëlle Mortier Vallat's collection on rue des Saints-Pères. *Clockwise, from top left:* A console in painted metal with a removable top made of travertine, a vase by René Butheau and painting by Marquet; a painting by Levy-Dhurmer above a card table by Ruhlmann; in the kitchen, a Russian armoire from the early 20th century, a lamp by Serrurier-Bovy, and silver by Jansen and Christofle (c. 1900); a neoclassic drawing and a 19th-century lecture lamp with a shade of pleated silk.
Right: In a small living room above a mantel painted in trompe-l'oeil leopard, a stuffed bison head dominates the room. The photos of Indian chiefs are by Curtis (mid 19th century).

1

STROLLING THROUGH
SAINT-GERMAIN-DES-PRĒS

1. MARE NOSTRUM *The restaurant specializes in fish dishes and dates back to the 1930-40s era. The decor from that period by Cocteau, Bérard and Vertès has been restored.*
2, place de l'Odéon, 75006.
Phone: +33 1 43 26 02 30.

2. HUMEURS *Despite its austere look, this is one of the most prestigious stores in the area.*
3, rue de l'Université, 75007.
Phone: +33 1 42 86 89 11.

3. DAVID HICKS FRANCE
A particular modern English style from the 1960s adapted here to that of the Left Bank bourgeoisie.
12, rue de Tournon, 75006.
Phone: +33 1 55 42 82 82.

4. CAP SHORE *In this temple of tableware, the dishes and accessories balance one's taste with one's purse.*
16, rue de Lille, 75007.
Phone: +33 1 49 27 90 00.

5. MURIEL GRATEAU *The designer of this site has pushed the art of detail to the point of perfection; pure lines, muted colors—with just a few things she says a lot.*
37, rue de Beaune, 75007.
Phone: +33 1 40 20 42 82.

**6 & 7. PLACE DE L'ODÉON
AND THÉÂTRE DE L'EUROPE**
All around the Théâtre de l'Europe, built by Peyre de Wally, an exemplary arched circle from the end of the neoclassic 18th century. Here one can escape from the crowds of the Latin Quarter.

8. PIERRE BURG *Passed down from father to son, this business makes superb*

garden ornaments in terracotta and ceramic, but their specialty is trompe-l'oeil.
Espace Buffon, 27, rue Buffon, 75005.
Phone: +33 1 47 07 06 79.

9. FABIENNE VILLACRÉCÈS *From pillows embroidered with sequins to necklaces made of pearl-gray Venetian glass, this designer ignores fashion in order to make the most of the styles from the turn of the last century.*
18, rue du Pré-aux-Clercs, 75007.
Phone: +33 1 45 49 24 84.

10. DEMEURE EN VILLE *We love the Swedish aesthetic, lamps from the 1930s and 1940s and creations by Mathias, Leguennec or Aubagnac. The latest novelties from the Design House Stockholm, and ceramics by Asa Lindström.*
23, rue Jacob, 75006
Phone: +33 1 56 24 96 04.

11. FRANCO MARIA RICCI *The famous Italian bookseller puts the same refinement and preciosity in the decor of his bookstores as he does in the pages of his beautiful books.*
189, boulevard Saint-Germain, 75007.
Phone: +33 1 45 49 10 94.

12. SAINT-SULPICE CHURCH *Symbol of the "Saint-Sulpician style" of art because of the vendors of religious souvenirs who in the past swarmed the area, some of whom remain today. It is also one of the largest Baroque churches in the capital.*

13. LIBRAIRIE DU MONITEUR
Everything you ever wanted to know about world architecture from any era can be found in this bookstore.
7, place de l'Odéon, 75006.
Phone: +33 1 44 41 15 75.

4

5

7

10   11

2

3

6

8   **9**

12   **13**

PLACE SAINT-GERMAIN
THE LOUIS VUITTON BOUTIQUE

Interior decorator Anouska Hempel created the decor for the Boutique Vuitton in Saint-Germain-des-Prés. Old trunks, the smell of wax and exotic perfumes, all compete to create the incomparable atmosphere of a long ocean voyage.
Left: This stained mahogany writing desk has unusual vertical drawers.
Right: The space is arranged in such a way that the luggage appears to be furniture. The suspended lamp is made of black rubber. The table dates from the 1940s.

Left: An imposing bookcase with wire-net doors punctuated by stucco half-columns (Oberlé-Laurent). On the desk a quilted tablecloth from Provence, a crystal girandole in the style of Louis XIV and a bronze vase converted into a lamp.

Below: On the mantel, 19th-century photos and a zebu tusk serve to augment the exotic flavor around a mirror that reflects a maharajah painting (Rajastan).

CLASSIC OR EXOTIC

A GLOBE-TROTTER'S BACHELOR PAD

Near the Seine at the house of decorator Tino Zervudachi, a mixture of objects found while bargain hunting at flea markets and on his many travels.
Above: The living room is in the Directoire style.
Center: In the office, functional furniture from the 1930s. The two mirrors and the rug are based on a design by Zervudachi.
Below: The bedroom overlooks a sunlit courtyard.
Right: The dining room, located between the entrance and the bedroom, is functional for any occasion.

REAR WINDOWS

Above: Agnès Comar has taken over these buildings with glass facades overlooking an old cobbled courtyard in the faubourg Saint-Germain. Once you've passed through the double door that leads to the courtyard, two ecru-colored raw linen curtains with black borders help give the feeling of being in a living room whose "ceiling" is the open sky. *Right page:* Above the table in the kitchen-dining room are three identical lanterns made of a striped fabric with trimmings (Thomas Boog). The table runner and plates were designed by Agnès Comar. Painted-wood mirrors reflect the building's glass facade. *Next pages:* A winter garden living room, designed by architect Anne-Cécile Comar allows the courtyard to become part of the house itself. On the right, a gold-leaf cat and two Zulu bridal headdresses rest on a lacquered Japanese table.

STROLLING THROUGH MONTPARNASSE

1. LA MAISON-ATELIER DE ROBERT COUTURIER *One of the last artists to witness the quarter's heyday, the sculptor worked here until the end of his life. His studio is just steps away from the Parc Montsouris.*

2. LES ATELIERS DE JEAN PERZEL *In this atelier, founded in 1923, the craftmanship still lives up to its original slogan: tradition and perfection. It is the Rolls Royce of art deco light fixtures.*
3, rue de la Cité-Universitaire, 75014.
Phone: +33 1 45 88 77 24.

3. FRANÇOIS HUBERT, HORLOGER-PENDULIER *What is more challenging than repairing or restoring an antique clock? Here, there is a solution for everything; some rare pieces are even for sale.*
43, rue Madame, 75006.
Phone: +33 1 45 44 22 00.

4. HÔTEL SAINTE-BEUVE *A small, charming place to meet only steps away from the Vavin intersection.*
9, rue Sainte-Beuve, 75006.
Phone: +33 1 45 48 20 07.

5. LA COUPOLE *All the great celebrities from the 1930s to the 1970s have shown up here at one time or another. The historic decor, now restored to its original glory, is well worth seeing.*
102, boulevard du Montparnasse, 75014.
Phone: +33 1 43 20 14 20.

6 & 8. LUCIEN PAYE RESIDENCE *The Lucien Paye residence is an architectural melting pot—a must-see in the neighborhood. Photos 6 and 8 show examples of exotic door handles and a period bas relief.*
45, boulevard Jourdan, 75014.
Phone: +33 1 53 80 75 75.

7. LA CITÉ INTERNATIONALE UNIVERSITAIRE *The university's international building, inaugurated in 1936, houses a remarkable library, as well as foreign students.*
19, boulevard Jourdan, 75014.
Phone: +33 1 43 13 65 96.

9. THE OBSERVATOIRE DE PARIS, *opened by Louis XIV in 1667, is still in use and is fascinating to visit.*
61, avenue de l'Observatoire, 75014.
Phone: +33 1 40 51 22 21.

5

8   **9**

BOURGEOIS-BOHEMIAN CHARM

This artist's studio is compact, but still reflects all the bourgeois-bohemian charm of Montparnasse.
Above: In the office, that occupies a corner of the living room, is a pastel by Leon Lhermitte and a wash drawing by J.-B. Huet sits on an easel. The art nouveau-style armchair is English.
Middle: In the entrance, a Regency umbrella stand and a stepladder discovered at the flea market. The portrait is of the owner's grandfather.
Below: A reverse shot of the corner office.
Right: In this bedroom, under a mansard roof, the drawings and landscapes are English. The bed linens are embroidered and come from the flea market at Saint-Ouen. A favorite resting place for Phillips the cat.

ROBERT COUTURIER'S STUDIO-HOME

Just steps away from the Parc Montsouris, this student of Maillol pursued his art with sensitivity, discipline and humor.

Above: In the living room, furniture from the 17th century — referred to as the "sheepbone" style — with natural slipcovers. Seen here from the back, is a Couturier sculpture from 1950 titled *Fillette sautant à la corde* .

Right: On the desk in Couturier's bedroom, the sculpture *Amandine* (1984), and on a nearby shelf rests *La Fillette au cerceau* (1952).

Right page: A view of the garden with (from left to right) *La Pensée* (1948), *Janus* (1950), *La Jeune Fille lamelliformée* (1950) and *Août 1996*. On the table, *17 ans ou l'adolescent* and *Moitié de couple* (1981). The collected works of a prolific life.

A GARRET UNDER THE MANSARD ROOF

A beautiful light illuminates these cozy rooms, which architect Laurent Bourgois transformed into a discretely luxurious nest. In the corner of the living room the couches are covered in flannel by Pierre Frey with kilim-covered throw pillows. On the 1960s coffee table is displayed a collection of Bakelite, wood and ivory balls. In the foreground, a duck by Lalanne.

INDUSTRIAL MATERIALS FOR MODERN ELEGANCE

Nathalie Decoster, who sculpts people in motion, loves the contrast of black and gray steel against white walls.
Above: In the living room, furniture in leather and metal and a reissued Godin stove. In the foreground, a piece by Nathalie titled *L'Air du temps.*
Right: Light colored wood lends an airiness to the bedroom of a contemporary woman who enjoys gazing at the fire from her bed.
Right page: For this artist's kitchen only professional equipment. The country table is made of old oak planks, and the stackable armchairs are a 1940s design reissued by Habitat.

Sixty years ago, the Japanese painter Foujita lived and worked here. Now restored, this retreat still carries with it memories of the 1920s when Montparnasse was in its heyday. *Below:* Ordered chaos dominates this book-lover's bedroom; the armchair is by Le Corbusier, the lithograph is by Hartung. *Right:* The old studio, as seen from above. The mezzanine is now a kitchen-dining room with a table by Knoll; the copper fish is by Lalanne.

IN FOUJITA'S FOOTSTEPS

HOME AMERICAN-STYLE

A studio atmosphere, with a love for all things American. This historic abode has seen George Sand and other renowned artists and craftsmen pass through.
Above: For a group of Parisian artists who love to relax, an old linden tree in the courtyard fills their summers with fragrance and provides plenty of shade.

Left: A jazz trio and singer (American, 1940s).
Right, above: In the foreground, the opposite of a torso painted in the style of Magritte by Charles Matton. On the wall, a sign for an old English pub.
Right, below: In a corner of this white-paneled retreat, the staircase leads to a mezzanine.

A GARDEN RETREAT

Here, in the Parc Montsouris, a grand view of what must be one of the most beautiful open spaces in Paris. This country-like corner provides the perfect retreat for work and for dreaming. The park itself is a paradise for children and for poets.

from the MARAIS
to the MADELEINE

Long ago, a famous omnibus linked the Bastille—that ancient fortress which was later so unceremoniously destroyed—to the Madeleine, an ornate temple dedicated to the glory of Napoleon's army. Just as the Bastille later became a prison, the Napoleonic temple eventually became the church it is today. King Louis Philippe dreamed of transforming the Madeleine into Paris's first train station. But in 1837, it was finally determined that the first Paris-Saint-Germain train, bellowing smoke as it went, would instead originate at Saint-Lazare. The train station's location, the train line itself and the rather haphazard expansion of this section of Paris were all part of the big push westward. It was as if a movement in this direction would allow the fresh winds from Deauville or Dieppe to dispel the smog that cloaked the capital.

Today, despite successive upheavals, those living on the Right Bank—undoubtedly shrewder than those inhabiting the other side of the Seine—remain very attached to the old historic buildings in their arrondissement. This is especially true of the 19th century dwellings—now 200 years old and by far the most romantic feature of this area. But what distinguishes the Right Bank most of all is the demographic detachment of its people. In the 1970s, it was *de rigour* among the Right Bank bourgeoisie to go slumming in Saint-Germain, with all its plotting and insurrections. Then there was the exodus from the center of the city to the suburbs, where urbanites sought open spaces and an escape from the endless expansion of office buildings into the area. Finally, there was a general push toward the west—Trocadéro, the Bois de Boulogne, Neuilly, even as far as the heights of Saint-Cloud—by well-to-do families seeking manor houses.

Of the million inhabitants who lived between the 1st and the 11th arrondissements in 1954, only 600,000 still remained at the end of the 20th century; a decrease of 42%. During the same time period, the number of people living in the 11th arrondissement was three times greater than that of the 8th arrondissement, where in 1954, the ratio had been 1 to 2*. This evolution, which appears even now to continue unabated,

Left:
The Place des Vosges.

Next spread:
1. The hôtel de Sully.
2. The Centre Georges Pompidou.
3. The Conservatoire National des Arts et Métiers.
4. The Eglise Saint-Eustache.
5. The Place des Victoires.
6. The Marché Saint-Honoré.
7. The Galerie Vivienne.

from the MARAIS

empties the heart of a city through its lack of concern for its citizens—whether they are ecological or didactic concerns. Singles, who are often trendsetters, are the people who mostly inhabit the center of Paris. They have reinvested in a district besieged all day and all week by the service industry. They have renovated apartments that once belonged to the upper middle class and have invested in former warehouses and converted them into lofts.

Although central to Parisian business activity, the Madeleine still falls within the sphere of influence of the Beaux Quartiers, where it sits imposingly among sandstone buildings whose facades tantalize the real estate brokers. In contrast, the Place de la Bastille opens out onto a neighborhood of factory workers and artisans. It is a place where many a revolt evolved into a revolution. The Bastille-Madeleine route links two worlds where the rich and poor, factory workers and financiers, blue and white collar workers each look upon the other with suspicion. These two important neighborhoods, where cohabitation is lived out at arm's length, are both an integral part of the complex fabric that is Paris.

Over the years, the Grands Boulevards that connect these two historic bastions have remained basically unchanged, at least in their liveliness and traffic jams. The boulevards form an arc that follows the ruins of the encircling wall built by Charles V at the end of the

14th century—a wall later fortified by Louis XIII in the 16th century, which passes through the archways of Saint-Martin and Saint-Denis built by Louis XIV. Beyond the arc lie the working-class areas; villages and small clusters of houses that were not incorporated into the city until the mid-19th century. There is no better place to observe this route than from the crescent-moon-shaped beltway that surrounds these ancient districts of Paris. From the Marais to Saint-Honoré, we can almost see the different layers of "skin" that make up the city. La Villette, Barbès, Pigalle, La Ville-l'Evêque. Like the opposition of north and south, the Left Bank and the Right Bank—this area forms the capital's east-west axis.

Over time, the Boulevard evolved into the

* These figures come from *Paris Mosaïque*, by Michel Pinçon and Monique Pinçon-Charlot, Ed. Calmann-Lévy, Paris 2001.

to the MADELEINE

Grands Boulevards, which Yves Montand made famous in his song, "I love to stroll along the grands boulevards. There are so many things, so many things to see!" Later on, via Place de la République, the boulevards became the axis for union rallies and demonstrations.

Perpendicular to the Grands Boulevards are the boulevards Sébastopol and Strasbourg that, attached end to end, serve to lengthen the boulevard Saint-Michel. Here, students mix with immigrants from the Goutte-d'Or region of Paris. Although Paris is neatly divided into "arrondissements" or districts—like a pie cut into equal parts—not all of the

districts are valued equally. What are considered fashionable districts today may not be tomorrow. And, according to Parisians, there are also districts to avoid. Those living in the 8th arrondissement are well aware of what distinguishes them from their fellow Parisians living in the 19th. Some who inhabit the 18th arrondissement may go so far as to differentiate themselves from neighbors living only yards away. There are even streets and avenues where one side of the street is favored over the other—usually based upon which side gets direct sunlight. And then there are those streets, like rue Saint-Florentin on the western edge of the 1st arrondissement, which has the east side of the street included in its jurisdiction, but not the west side.

In Paris, landmarks that help define the spirit of each district consistently punctuate the east-west axis from Place de la Bastille, to Place de la Madeleine. Place des Vosges, Place de l'Opéra, Place de la République, Place de la Concorde and Place Vendôme are the most famous. Each represents something different: the area surrounding Place des Victoires, known long ago for the production of upholstery fabric, and was later pretty much abandoned. The area saw new life when the famous fashion designer Kenzo moved there in the 1970s, ten years later he was joined by other fashion designers. Les Halles, which had become an urban blight, was completely transformed. In the Marais, beautiful hôtels particuliers built in the 16th and 17th centuries provide a contrast to the townhouses of the Left Bank. As of late, the prestige of the 3rd arrondissement has risen greatly due in part to the presence of the Picasso Museum which opened there in 1985, and the numerous contemporary art galleries. Living in the Marais district today is almost like joining a religious sect where a certain image is strictly observed. Beyond the Bastille, the faubourg Saint-Antoine is also being rediscovered and reinvented. Everywhere one looks—above, beyond and all around Paris's 20 districts, in areas still disdained by many—one can feel a new sense of vibrancy and life. More likely than not, it is from these new frontiers that the newest ideas in decorating will come.

Thanks to an eclectic auctioneer, a museum-like amalgam of periods and styles enlivens this 17th-century townhouse in the heart of the Marais. *Above:* In the entrance, a pair of stenciled columns surrounds a fresco mural of Hercules by Farnèse.

A CROSS-CULTURAL MIX OF PERIODS AND STYLES

Below: In a corner of the living room a Kota reliquary made of wood and copper contrasts with an art deco Syrian vase. The portrait is by Morvan (1960).
Right: Interconnecting rooms open onto the garden. The double doors are painted in faux mahogany and the moldings are accented with gold leaf.

STROLLING THROUGH THE MARAIS

1. SQUARE LÉOPOLD-ACHILLE
A peaceful location situated between the rue Payenne and rue de Sévigné.

2. LE PAVILLON DE LA REINE
Hidden behind an imposing building on the Place des Vosges, this graceful townhouse hotel is a haven of peace and tranquility, only steps away from the bustling activity of the district.
28, place des Vosges, 75003.
Phone: +33 1 40 29 19 19.

3. LES INDIENNES *Not a place for wild Indians, this boutique offers examples of a sophisticated art— 19th-century Indian cashmere shawls.*
10, rue Saint-Paul, 75004.
Phone: +33 1 42 72 35 34.

4. LES CARRELAGES DU MARAIS
Glazed terracotta tiles in any shape, color or size, from floor to ceiling. These tiles are the very best.
46, rue Vieille-du-Temple, 75004.
Phone: +33 1 42 78 17 43.

5. BERNIE *A mixture of period pieces and materials in the heart of an area that dates back to the 16th century. Here, only luxuries for the 21st century.*
12, rue de Sévigné, 75004.
Phone: +33 1 44 59 35 88.

6. GALERIE SENTOU *exhibits contemporary works that are both beautiful and stylish. This place practically defines creativity.*
18, rue du Pont-Louis-Philippe, 75004.
Phone: +33 1 42 77 44 79.

7 & 10. MUSÉE CARNAVALET *The setting of this museum devoted to the history of Paris is magnificent. Housed in three*
period townhouses, it is undoubtedly the most charming museum in the capital.
23, rue de Sévigné, 75004.
Phone: +33 1 44 59 58 58.

8. PLAISAIT *An illustrious Paris goldsmith since 1820, here one finds replicas of rare old pieces along with contemporary designs—all crafted with the greatest precision and artistry.*
9, place des Vosges, 75004.
Phone: +33 1 48 87 34 80.

9. MUSÉE PICASSO *During the time of Louis XIV, this townhouse was called "Salé," the home of a rich salt tax collector. Both the building and its contents are jewels of an area already glittering with architectural treasures.*
5, rue de Thorigny, 75003.
Phone: +33 1 42 71 25 21.

11. ARREDAMENTO
Devoted to contemporary design, this shop carries works by such illustrious names as Ettore Sottsass and Gilles Derain. The items date from the period between yesterday and tomorrow.
18, quai des Célestins, 75004.
Phone: +33 1 42 78 71 77.

12. LE GÉNIE DE LA BASTILLE
The French Revolution's ideals have never been portrayed so lightly.

13. IZRAËL *It's more than a grocery store; it's a museum. We would list this boutique for its scent alone. The variety of products in this shop makes it a genuine Promised Land.*
30, rue François-Miron, 75004.
Phone: +33 1 42 72 66 23.

1

6

7

10

2 3

4 5

8 9

11 12 13

WHERE ELEVATION MEETS SECLUSION

This space was created out of an old industrial building and has all of the dramatics of a loft, while still providing its occupants with their own private space. The master designer of this house, made entirely of wood, is the young architect Hervé Vermesch. Here in this ancient tannery, a perfect balance is achieved between the original structure and the new spaces.
Left: By removing a section of the roof, Vermesch made room for a private indoor garden.

Right: For the bathroom walls, plain white tiles and a sink made of a block of damascened stone (Robinetterie Chavonnet).

Below: In the kitchen, a soapstone worktable; the range hood is made of cathedral glass. All cabinetry is by Ikea. On the walls, sections of damascened stone.

Right page: The living room beams were exposed by the bachelor himself. In the background a partition separates the living room from the TV room. The central partition, with its built-in photos, was once a wall used for jai alai. It was found in a salvage shop.

STROLLING THROUGH THE MARAIS

1. KIMONOYA *K as in kimono, I as in Ikebana, M as in of the moment.... It has all the mystery of the Empire of the Rising Sun, falling somewhere between the traditional and the innovative. 11, rue du Pont-Louis-Philippe, 75004. Phone: + 33 1 48 87 30 24.*

2. LES MILLE FEUILLES *Flowers and other ephemeral objects live side-by-side in perfect harmony. A garden of the senses, fleeting yet always renewed by Pierre Brinon and Philippe Landri. 2, rue Rambuteau, 75003. Phone: + 33 1 42 78 32 93.*

3. MADE IN JAPAN MINIATURE *Here, everything comes from far off. An endless supply of exotic gifts. 11, rue de Béarn, 75003. Phone: + 33 1 42 77 03 63.*

4. GALERIE TAVOLA *Their specialty is table art. Connoisseurs come to find a rare and lovely assortment of wares from the great potters and ceramists of the 19th and 20th centuries. 19, rue du Pont-Louis-Philippe, 75004. Phone: + 33 1 42 74 20 24.*

5. MAISON LAURENÇAT *The ultimate in glass restoration and repair since 1894. New objects in glass can also be found in this studio-boutique devoted to fragile, beautiful works. 19, rue des Gravilliers, 75003. Phone: + 33 1 42 72 96 45.*

6. LE COMPTOIR DES ÉCRITURES *An exceptionally wide variety of paper, brushes and inks; a temple to calligraphy in the age of computers. 35, rue Quincampoix, 75004. Phone: + 33 1 42 78 95 10.*

7. GALERIE FIFTEASE *This gallery pays homage to the 1950s, dedicating itself exclusively to the French decorative arts. 7, rue du Perche, 75003. Phone: + 33 1 40 27 04 40.*

8. ENTRÉE DES FOURNISSEURS *Two thousand different varieties of buttons, an abundance of anything else one finds in a notions shop. 8, rue des Francs-Bourgeois, 75004. Phone: + 33 1 48 87 58 98.*

9. L'ESCARGOT MONTORGUEIL *In this, one of the oldest restaurants in les Halles, the decor vies with the food. In the entranceway a ceiling originally painted for Sarah Bernhardt's kitchen. A must-see. 38, rue Montorgueil, 75001. Phone: + 33 1 42 36 83 51.*

10. LE GEORGES *Named after the French President Georges Pompidou, founder of the Centre Pompidou, this restaurant atop the museum offers the perfect place to rest a while, with one of the most beautiful vistas of Paris. 19, rue Beaubourg, 75004. Phone: + 33 1 44 78 47 99.*

11. TEISSO ANTIQUITÉS *Airport terminal lamps by Jieldé, chairs by Cadestin de Bertoïa, a bed by Prouvé, armchairs by Eames....need we say more? 81, rue Vieille-du-Temple, 75003. Phone: + 33 1 48 04 59 07.*

12. MICHEL GERMOND *Whether the job takes 15 minutes or 1,500 hours, for Michel Germond, restorer and maker of fine furniture, each time it's a labor of love. To him, what matters most is the artistry and timelessness of each piece he makes. 78, quai de l'Hôtel-de-Ville, 75004. Phone: + 33 1 42 78 04 78.*

13. THE STAIRCASE OF THE HÔTEL LE PELETIER-SAINT-FARGEAU *All the nobility of the Age of Enlightenment can be found in this hotel, recently linked to the Carnavalet townhouse.*

14. AUX DEUX ORPHELINES *Don't let the name fool you—this store is full of treasures that are never homeless for long. 21, place des Vosges, 75004. Phone: + 33 1 42 72 63 97.*

1

5

6

9

11   **12**

2 3

4

7 8

10

13 14

THE PAST AND THE PRESENT

In this old apartment in the Marais, the owners mix a bit of everything—bric-à-brac, mirrors and works in wood. Despite the extreme contrasts they blend beautifully alongside important examples of modern art. An eclectic yet harmonious decor designed by Frédéric Méchiche. The living room is filled with woodwork from a stagecoach station dating back to the 18th century.

Who said the Directoire style wasn't compatible with a taste for the sporty?

Above: This black-and-white room is embellished by a work in black ink by painter Charles Blais; the delicate string of lights is from the Galerie Sentou. In the foreground, a plaster vase rests on a pedestal made of bleached pine.

Below: Frédéric Méchiche's workout room looks more like a salon; the wooden sculpture is by Sofu Teshigahara, the original plaster work is by Laszlo Szabo. Beneath an engraving by Pincermin, a compression sculpture by César.

Right: An unusual Directoire-style bathtub made of deep-gray painted sheet metal. The bathtub pedestal is made of stone; the decorative marble floor is from the 18th century.

THE BEAUTY OF TRUE SIMPLICITY

Decorator and designer Didier Gomez is very much at home in the Marais. He prefers simple forms, and likes the contrast between shadow and light. In his apartment, he has eliminated hallways to accentuate the open space. With an emphasis on symmetry, he has placed all of the doorways in the same line of vision. The panels are made of Wenge-wood, the hinges are mounted on linchpins. French windows provide a mixture of rusticity and refinement.

STROLLING THROUGH THE BASTILLE

1. L'ART DU TEMPS *Bird cages, curiosities in cast iron, an armadillo... this surreal inventory is as captivating as the Bastille itself.*
63, rue de Charonne, 75011.
Phone: + 33 1 47 00 29 30.

2. TROPICAL TRADING
A good place to rest a while while exploring the Bastille.
This ancestral stronghold represents the finest in Parisian craftsmanship.
23, rue Basfroi, 75011.
Phone: + 33 1 44 93 93 44.

3. FLORENCE DUFIEUX
She is wild about batiks and paints large motifs on silk, each a one-of-a-kind design to adorn screens, seats, trellises, slip covers, you name it.
9, rue de la Fontaine-au-Roi, 75011.
Phone: + 33 1 42 72 87 79.

4. LA QUINCAILLERIE AU PROGRÈS
Just about anything imaginable can be found in this paradise of a store, where time stands still. Established in 1873, it specializes in home furnishings for craftspeople or anyone who loves both the beautiful and the practical.
11 bis, rue Faidherbe, 75011.
Phone: + 33 1 43 71 70 61.

5. PASSAGE *One hundred different doors, from traditional to modern. As its name suggests, it is housed in an open space. An equally huge variety of door handles, both practical and decorative.*
9, rue Véga, 75012.
Phone: + 33 1 55 78 20 30.

6. LE MASSON BRUNOT *In this studio, painted furniture is not only restored, but returned to its original glory by owner Gwenola Masson.*
171, rue du Fbg-Saint-Antoine, 75011.
Phone: + 33 1 49 28 00 38.

7. GALERIE SÉGUIN
This man just loves the 1950s, and is an expert on furniture by Jean Prouvé:

he's held several exhibitions of Prouvé's work, and has published a remarkable catalogue on his oeuvre.
34, rue de Charonne, 75011.
Phone: + 33 1 48 06 10 66.
5, rue des Taillandiers, 75011.
Phone: + 33 1 47 00 32 35.

8. MAISON DELISLE *Here, all things luminous—from lamps to sconces to chandeliers—come to life. A distinguished member of the entrepreneurial Colbert Committee, he bases the designs for these beautiful lamps on antique models.*
4, rue du Parc-Royal, 75003.
Phone: + 33 1 42 72 21 34.

9. ARZINC, FRANCIS ARSÈNE
This one-time roofer has a passion for zinc. He makes amazing things out of the material that once graced Paris's rooftops, creating a wide variety of objects for the home.
196, boulevard de Charonne, 75020.
Phone: + 33 1 40 09 74 46.

10. FÉES D'HERBE *In this very civilized jungle, Sylvie Aubry and Dominique Bernard display their knowledge of interior decorating and their imaginations with panache.*
23, rue Faidherbe, 75011.
Phone: + 33 1 43 70 14 76.

11. SOUBRIER *This family den extends to several floors. The company, which rents items out to filmmakers, has accumulated over the last 150 years objects that they sometimes agree to part with but only with the greatest reluctance.*
14, rue de Reuilly, 75012.
Phone: + 33 1 43 72 93 71.

12. GALERIE OPALE *has dedicated itself exclusively to exhibiting writers' portraits. It is open to the public and sells portraits of these great men and women of letters, from Cocteau to Ellroy to Auster.*
8, rue Charlot, 75003.
Phone: + 33 1 40 29 93 33.

2 3

6

8

11 12

OFFICE ELEGANCE IN THE HEART OF PARIS

The internationally known decorator Alberto Pinto wanted to house his business in a typically Parisian house. He found the perfect atelier in the rear courtyard of this 17th-century townhouse, in a space measuring 3,600 square feet and covering four floors. Here Pinto exhibits his genius for the art of gracious living. *Below:* Plenty of glass overlooking a spacious courtyard. *Right:* The original stairwell was painted to look like stone. The chandelier is a 17th-century original.

In the atelier's central workroom, documentation of a huge variety of colors, fabrics and materials provide inspiration for future designs. Here assistants research the essential elements that will eventually result in a creation of distinction and flair.

Alberto Pintos's relaxed
conference room:
slipcovers on the
armchairs and sofa
are made of raw linen
(Pierre Frey), a rug
designed by Pinto for
Sam Laïk, a large
painting by Manolo
Valdès and chairs
and a round table
designed by Ed Tuttle.

Everyone who is anyone stays at the Ritz — Marcel Proust, Coco Chanel and Ernest Hemingway to name a few. Considered a temple to opulent accommodation, the Ritz houses hundreds of objects and antiques and is one of the most prestigious showplaces, for the most famous people in the world.
Clockwise, from top left: In the Windsor suite, everything must sparkle.
A detail of the ceiling in the Chopin suite.
In the attic, candelabras and lamp bases sit side by side with busts of Hemingway.
The swimming pool in the hotel's health club.
Right page: In the Vendôme salon the truly elegant take tea.

PLACE VENDÔME
IN THE WINGS AT THE RITZ

Left: These fanciful Indian cotton fabrics lend a certain whimsy and exoticism to this otherwise classic apartment. The drapes are by Braquenié and the objects are from the Paul Bert market. *Below:* On the mantel a pair of lamps by Nicole Mugler and a Chinese cup. Above, a classic Louis XVI gilded mirror. To the left, a series of four drawings in red chalk by Hubert Robert.

A PASSION FOR PRINTS

PALAIS-ROYAL

Right: This salon, tucked beneath a mansard roof, overlooks the Tuileries Gardens. The sofas and padded chairs are original Napoleon III (from the Drouot auction house); a romantic floral screen highlights a marble fireplace with a painting by Anne Vincent hanging above.
Below: A collection of gouaches depicting Chinese vases hang side-by-side on a large paisley-motif wallpaper (Rubelli). On the Louis XV armchair, fabric by Le Manach.

This small apartment with its stunning panoramic view, nestles under the eaves of a building on the corner of rue de Rivoli overlooking the Tuileries Gardens. Each element was chosen with the intention of showing the view to its greatest advantage. In the distance, the Jeu de Paume, the Invalides, the Eiffel Tower.

A PIED-Ā-TERRE IN THE SKY

Above: The padded leather armchair is by Yves Halard; the side table, lamp, fruit bowl, tray and the French quilted bedspread are by Blanc d'Ivoire.
Below: In the entranceway, the flooring is made of cement tiles; the clock and the sofa are from the era of Napoleon III, the mirror and the chest of drawers are in the Dutch style.
Right page: This apartment was originally an immense living room-dining room. Today, it's been transformed into a vast studio loft. Brick-colored walls lend a theatrical air to this garret space.

The Opera Garnier was first unveiled to the public at the 1867 World's Fair, and was officially inaugurated in 1875. Throughout the Second Empire, Charles Garnier hired only the very best artisans from each different guild to create this exquisite interior, with its gilded masks and garlands, bronzes, colored marble and red-velvet upholstery. At the turn of the 21st century — after two years of restoration — this sumptuous edifice has reclaimed all of its former splendor. A feast for the eyes, under a ceiling painted by Chagall (not shown). *Below:* The Opera's interior, as seen from the boxes. *Right:* A phalanx of the Opera's famous armchairs as far as the eye can see.

A NIGHT AT THE OPERA

CLASH OF STYLES, HARMONY OF TASTE

Interior decorators Maurice Savinel and Roland Le Bevillon have ingeniously mixed together objects which could be considered bourgeois with other more humble pieces. Put together with imagination and taste, this is a quintessentially Parisian apartment.
Above: Kitchen furniture designed by the decorators themselves.
Right: Through the doorway, we can just make out the dining room-kitchen.
Right page: In the living room, the couch, also designed by the owners, is covered in a prune-colored velvet (Pierre Frey). On the art deco-inspired rug sit taborets made of ironwood from Burma. In the background, two plaster columns flank a piece of Chinese furniture, above which hangs a 1940 oil painting by Soungourof.

1

STROLLING THROUGH THE PALAIS-ROYAL

1. SOFITEL DEMEURE HOTEL CASTILLE
At this private hotel near Place Vendôme—where Cocteau once lived—we find an elegant intimacy. Jacques Grange's redecoration exudes a sense of warmth and comfort.
37, rue Cambon, 75001.
Phone: + 33 1 44 58 44 58.

2. SALONS DU PALAIS-ROYAL SHISEIDO
Designed by perfumer Serge Lutens, these mauve and plum colored salons give off a hint of the fragrances found within.
25, rue de Valois, 75001.
Phone: + 33 1 49 27 09 09.

3. GALERIE COLBERT
Built in 1826, it was once a high-society gathering place. Today, it is a modest, charming passageway between the Palais-Royal and the Bibliothèque Nationale.

4. DIDIER LUDOT *He knows the art of transforming secondhand clothes into works of art, or at least very wearable fashions. An antiques dealer who specializes in dresses, he investigates grandmothers' closets and resells the contents to their granddaughters. Clever!*
24, galerie de Montpensier, 75001.
Phone: + 33 1 42 96 06 56.

5. CAFÉ DE L'ÉPOQUE *Just a simple bistro except for its unusual charm and its upper-crust clientele. Situated at the entrance of the marvelous Véro-Dodat passageway.*
2, rue du Bouloi, 75001.
Phone: + 33 1 42 33 40 70.

6. LE GRAND VÉFOUR *This temple to gourmet cooking maintained the*

marvelous decor that brought it from the early 19th century—when Balzac was writing A Harlot High and Low.
17, rue du Beaujolais, 75001.
Phone: + 33 1 42 96 56 27.

7 & 12. THE GARDENS OF THE PALAIS-ROYAL *As soon as the weather breaks, businessmen from the surrounding area enjoy a sandwich here at noon, and the birds eat the crumbs. In modern-day Paris, there is no place quite as convivial.*

8. MARCHÉ SAINT-HONORÉ
The old market's iron arcades have been replaced by an impressive structure of glass and steel designed by Ricardo Bofill. This, one of his most beautiful constructions, is Bofill at his best.
6, rue du Marché-Saint-Honoré, 75001.

9. LE PRINCE JARDINIER *A descendent of the illustrious Broglie family, the owner sells a variety of garden implements that carry his own label.*
37, rue de Valois, 75001.
Phone: + 33 1 42 60 37 13.

10. LA VIE DE CHÂTEAU *Jean de Rohant-Chabot was bored with the business world, so he opened this store for rare and valuable tableware. For those living the good life, it is a mandatory destination.*
17, rue de Valois, 75001.
Phone: + 33 1 49 27 09 82.

11. LA GALERIE DE VALOIS
Built by Victor Louis for Philippe d'Orléans—the first real estate deal—this prominent Parisian building remains one of the most charming places in the heart of the capital to stroll past.

4

5

7

9

10

11

6

8

2   **3**

12

Left: There's a romantic feeling to this living room created out of a hallway. The long tablecloths help define the space, while identical table treatments create a mirroring effect. The mahogany chairs are in the 19th-century Russian style. The hanging oil lamps are made of sheet metal. On each table a small pagoda made by master craftsmen. In the background, a 17th-century portrait of an English gentleman.
Below: A hallway is cleverly transformed into a photo gallery. On the fabric-covered divider, "Retour d'Egypte" (Braquenié), and a four-leaf clover by Louise de Vilmorin.

LIFE BY LENGTH

Right Bank style: Above an English table, an oil painting by Garel surrounded by lesser masters of the 19th century.

Interconnecting living rooms with a prominently displayed portrait by Christian Bérard.

IN A WRITER'S HOME

In Paris each
arrondissement can be
viewed as a village with
a distinct personality
all its own, where
people of discernment
can choose their location
according to taste and
temperament. Writer
Marie-France Pochna
chose this distinguished
residence near the Place
des Victoires. Here she
cultivates a mixture of
styles, while at the same
time clearly defining her
own. In the living room,
the walls are floor-to-
ceiling bookshelves.
The two facing sofas are
by Dominique Kieffer.
The screen is by David
Webster, the table is
from the 1940s, and the
Egyptian stool is a
contemporary piece.

Below: An unlikely encounter between a bathtub and a leather Chesterfield couch. The stool is Egyptian and the cabochon goblets are in the baroque style.

Right: In this kitchen-dining room the table is set with porcelain dishes designed by Raymond Loewy for Rosenthal.

A BOOKSTORE THAT'S NOT BY THE BOOK

Frédéric Castaing collects and sells notable letters, manuscripts, autographs, dedications and photos from such diverse characters as Francis I to the French actress Arletty.
Above: Claude Monet at Giverny, shown here alongside one of his letters.
Right: This handsome shop, that overlooks the Palais-Royal Gardens, has a subdued and distinguished atmosphere befitting its merchandise.
Right page: The guardian of this establishment, with its wall-to-wall framed pictures, likes to evoke a sense of nostalgia by pairing letters with a photo of their author—putting a name with a face, so to speak.

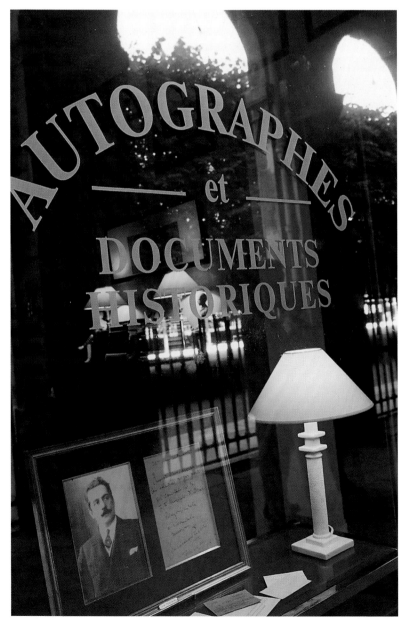

TROMPE-L'OEIL ELEGANCE

In an unusual touch Anne Gayet commissioned Nathalie Mahiu to paint the walls of this cozy living room to resemble woodwork. The sofa's white-cotton slipcover is by Rebecca Campeau; cashmere kilim rugs and a romantic day bed, all serve to recreate the eclecticism of 19th-century Paris.

These days eat-in kitchens are no longer the exception but the rule. Here, a dining room with a kitchen alcove. Both the original molding and the fireplace, dating back to the early 19th century, were restored. A quilt from Provence and rattan chairs, a chandelier and a wicker tea cart harmonize in this small room.

The Hôtel Costes, redecorated by Jacques Garcia, has become one of the most fashionable hotels in Paris. In spite of its diminutive size, the ambiance is warm and welcoming—a comfortable haven at the corner of the Place Vendôme. The decor is completely original with comfortable upholstered chairs and flea-market finds, creating a bohemian-style elegance. It's this combination of imagination and chic that attracts clients weary of the usual decor one finds in luxury hotels.

PLACE VENDÔME
A SMALL LUXURY HOTEL

Above: In the courtyard, two large stone porticos support antique statues in the neoclassic style.
Below, left: In the entrance, velvet consoles are sheathed in studded fabric.
Below right, and right page, bottom: Jacques Garcia used antique furniture both for the bathrooms and the private rooms (here, neo-Indo-Portuguese from the time of Napoleon III), but not in the capacity for which they were originally intended.
Right page, top: In one of the living rooms, a framed herbarium.
A Napoleon III-style sofa was redesigned according to the patterns from that time.

Pastel tones, a collection of whimsical drawings from the turn of the century, souvenirs and mementoes create a soft, feminine ambiance, reminiscent of a young Parisian girl's room at the turn of the century.
Left: On the walls of this salon wide pine paneling painted in pale tones, a collection of pastels and "three-pencil" drawings by Helleu blend right in.
Below: Here, a collection of decorative vases where works by Daum, Galée and Lalique mingle with less valuable works.

FROM THE DAYS OF THE BELLE ÉPOQUE

FAUBOURG SAINT-HONORÉ

Right: In this living room in the 8th arrondissement, the exposed beams have been painted glossy white. A handsome Louis XVI chest of drawers and a sleek roll-top desk from the 19th century blend well with the chairs' clean white slipcovers.
Below: A collection of small clocks and old watches positioned around an alabaster vase converted into a lamp. In the foreground, a glass inkwell.

STROLLING DOWN THE FAUBOURG AND THE RUE SAINT-HONORĒ

1. HERMÈS *The most distinguished leather-works store in the Faubourg, now offers an extensive collection of household items. Watch who comes and goes during the holidays and you'll see a very wide range of the privileged class.*
24, rue du Faubourg-Saint-Honoré, 75008. Phone: + 33 1 40 74 61 00.

2. GRANGE *Comfort, tradition and style define this establishment that gives the flavor of an old family home.*
5, place Saint-Augustin 75008.
Phone: + 33 1 45 22 07 72.

3. GALERIE ARIANE DANDOIS
This merchant recently opened her store of beautiful, decorative furniture at Place Beauvau.
92, rue du Faubourg-Saint-Honoré, 75008. Phone: + 33 1 43 12 39 39.

4. JACQUES PERRIN *Some furniture of 18th-century aristocrats and financiers of the Age of Enlightenment is displayed here in a discrete and harmonious fashion. The overall atmosphere is one of unquestionable quality.*
98, rue du Faubourg-Saint-Honoré, 75008. Phone: + 33 1 42 65 01 38.

5. GALERIE AVELINE *If the objects and furniture here weren't so rare and so expensive, we'd encourage everyone to visit this gallery where everything is both enchanting and exceptional, and often amusing. The "curator," Jean-Marie Rossi, is himself an international star. We visit him as we would a frequently discussed, rare historical monument.*
94, rue du Faubourg-Saint-Honoré, 75008. Phone: + 33 1 42 66 60 29.

6 & 7. FRETTE *Not simply sheets and bedding here, but the most opulent and voluptuous bedroom accessories imaginable.*

49, rue du Faubourg-Saint-Honoré, 75008. Phone: + 33 1 42 66 47 70.

8. HÔTEL ASTOR *Removed from the hustle and bustle of the city, yet centrally located. Frédéric Méchiche redecorated this luxury hotel in the style of the late 1930s.*
11, rue d'Astorg, 75008.
Phone: + 33 1 53 05 05 05.

9. COLETTE *Simply the place to shop or just visit. No further explanation needed. Colette is a phenomenon; that is its greatness and its limitation.*
213, rue Saint-Honoré, 75001.
Phone: + 33 1 55 35 33 90.

10. THE RITZ *The reception and service one receives here is unsurpassed in all of Paris. Designed to please the rich and the powerful, one can still have lunch or tea here for a reasonable price.*
15, place Vendôme, 75001.
Phone: + 33 1 43 16 30 30.

11. PLACE VENDÔME *is a masterwork by Hardouin-Mansart, architect to Louis XIV. A statue of the King once stood center square. The column that replaced the monarch's statue is made from cannons used at the battle of Austerlitz.*

12. LA MADELEINE *Built by Napoleon as a temple to the glory of his armies, the chic now come to this church to get married. It matches the neoclassic style of the Assemblée Nationale.*

13. KUGEL *This store harbors treasures that even a millionaire couldn't collect. To this day, two brothers continue to research their treasures, just as earlier generations of their family researched treasures before them.*
279, rue Saint-Honoré, 75008.
Phone: + 33 1 42 60 86 23.

2 3

4

5

8

10

12 13

NATURALISM IN THE ART DECO STYLE

Thomas Boog, the grand master of shell collecting, is also an amateur collector of Oriental art and hunting trophies. A prolific traveler and explorer, his shop and his apartment are filled with the spoils of his travels. The settees are by Le Corbusier, the chairs by Eames, the zebra skin is from South Africa, a Chinese-style clock was designed by Boog himself, and the antlers come from an Egyptian buffalo.

FAUBOURG SAINT-HONORÉ

Right: A tableau of objects against a background of enlarged botanical reproductions.
Below: In this room, a 19th-century silk-embroidered wall hanging; the lantern is by Thomas Boog.
Right page: The ambiance of this room evokes the Far East, with its mixture of Chinese furniture and lacquered objects. The hanging lamp is made of white silk; the candlestick holder of wrought iron in a coral design was created by the master of the house.

BEATAE · MARIAE · VIRGINI · LAVRETANAE

from MONTMARTRE
to the BEAUX QUARTIERS

n 1860, Montmartre—the hill that dominates Paris, with its vineyards, windmills and garrets—was annexed to Paris, along with a myriad of other outlying villages that stretched from Passy to La Villette. Among all of them, however, it was Montmartre that stood out. The statesman Georges Clemenceau was once the mayor of this community—a place where the inhabitants leave their enclave with great reluctance, and only when obliged to do something in the city.

No one passes *through* Montmartre; one goes right *to* it. Montmartre is reached by way of a network of small streets that Edith Piaf immortalized in song. Today, the steep staircases are just as difficult to climb as they always were, but maneuvering cars on this hillside—transformed long ago by a flood into a veritable mount—poses a whole different set of problems. The Sacré-Coeur basilica with its imposing white dome tops Montmartre and dwarfs the jumble of historic, slate-gray houses nearby that people will snap up at any price. Montmartre is like a fortified city, an entrenched camp with even its own cable car that lords over the bustling boulevards below. Isolated as it may be, few districts are as linked to the legend of Paris as Montmartre. All true Parisians carry a piece of Montmartre in their soul. The feeling of solidarity with Montmartre radiates far beyond the district itself—this "island" has over time represented independence, insurrection, bohemia and the simple pleasures of life. At the turn of the 20th century, it also became a cradle of modern art. One can imagine la Goulue, the cabaret dancer made famous by Toulouse-Lautrec, crossing paths with Picasso's *Demoiselles d'Avignon*, Manet's top hats and Poulbot's blue-collar workers.

The slopes that begin at the Sacré-Coeur de Jésus and run down to Bonne Nouvelle and Montmartre's huge fabric store, the Marché Saint-Pierre, down to the Galeries Lafayette are very long. It's only when we near Pigalle, Trinité and Nouvelle Athènes on the side of Notre-Dame-de-Lorette and over to the Opera, that we once again come upon those kinds of old buildings with modest, melancholy facades. Many of them recall Paris's

Left:
Notre-Dame-de-Lorette (early 19th century), and the basilica of the Sacré-Coeur.

Next spread:
1. The Place Saint-Georges.
2. The Musée de la Vie Romantique.
3. The Passage Jouffroy and bargain bookstores.
4. The Cité Trévise.
5. The Hôtel Vernet's dining room, on the street with the same name (16th arrondissement).
6. The Musée d'Art Moderne, built in the 1930s, now renamed the Palais de Tokyo.
7. The Cité Léandre.
8. Place de l'Alma, the flame here is the same size as on the French Statue of Liberty, by Bartholdi.

from MONTMARTRE

romantic period when tragedians, orientalist painters, bohemians in love with young shop girls, powerful financiers or those on the brink of success…an entire cast of characters out of some Balzacian play resided behind the neoclassic walls of Montmartre.

The first houses in Montmartre were built cheaply and quickly by factory workers who came, for the most part, from Limousin. Originally built to house the more modest elements of society, they were nevertheless dependable and worthy of the prestigious sandstone of which they were built. In general, they are attractive, modestly proportioned 18th-century-style buildings, reminiscent of a time when life was so much simpler. Their interiors too are modest, with none of those frenzied patterns found on stucco walls. Often the only decoration on these houses is latticework window sills, a few serrated cornices, an ancient porch here a stone post there, and quaint lanterns made of sheet metal. But what history! Behind the old cast-iron fountain, there is a tree so old that it must remember having seen Rubempré and Coralie, Balzac's star-crossed lovers*, passing by. Farther west is the Quartier l'Europe where trains from the station at Saint-Lazare (named after an ancient prison for women) carried the first Impressionist painters, eager to paint in the *plein air* genre, out towards Saint-Germain-en-Laye. The trains also carried those first tourists, also desirous of taking in the fresh air.

From the Quartier l'Europe, we move on to the Beaux Quartiers, the most exclusive sections of Paris, situated in the westernmost part of the city which includes the 16th, 17th, 7th and 8th arrondissements, as well as Neuilly-sur-Seine. The people who live here are not

exactly what you would call defenders of a particular aesthetic, but compared to all the other denizens of Paris, who derive their identity from its history a legend or from their geographical placement, the people here (who came to refer to the buildings in this area, almost all constructed in one fell swoop, as Paris's "Haussmanian" district) base their traditions on a particular state of mind, rather than on anything they've inherited. The idea here, basically, is to live among one's own.

In 1826, a finance company mapped out a new group of streets

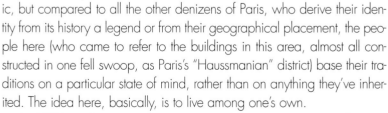

* Honoré de Balzac, *A Harlot High and Low*, 1838-1847.

to the BEAUX QUARTIERS

which would fan out in the pattern of a star across what was still then the countryside. All the streets intersected at Place de l'Europe and each street was named after a European capital in what was to be a congenial collaboration of cosmopolitanism established on an architectural plan. The Boulevard Malesherbes plows through a

network of interwoven streets. Its temperament is slightly different than bohemian Montmartre, the light-heartedness of Pigalle, or the very respectable 17th arrondissement— where, many years ago, loose women discreetly entertained the wealthy tenants living on the ground floor. (These women now go by other names, but the Beaux Quartiers are still full of them.) On the second and third floors of these buildings lived famous doctors who received their guests in those bourgeois apartments with all their vast connecting rooms; like Doctor Proust, for example, who lived on rue de Courcelles, and was father to one particular Marcel. Above them, members of the middle middle class resided, and one floor above that lived members of the lower classes. Finally, in tiny rooms just under the eaves of the building, lived the maids, who were relegated to using the back stairs to empty the chamber pots.

Today, these houses have been transformed into comfortable apartments. Finally freed from the influence of their elders, the younger generation of Parisians has invested a great deal here. If one finds a place that isn't exactly one's style, all that's required is imagination. Dare to diverge from the beaten path and you can successfully turn your place into "Home,

Sweet Home." Paris was once very structured—different sections of the city, it was understood, housed different kinds of people. Today all of that has changed. Places once considered "out of the loop," too "historical" or "bourgeois" are now considered fair game. Despite its propensity for classification, Paris still remains a city where anything is possible, as long as imagination reigns.

NEW LIFE FOR AN OLD STUDIO

Two young architects took a whole new look at this artist's house located at the foot of the hill Montmartre. They tore down the walls and ceiling to maximize both light and space. *Left:* In the garden patio, the main pathway is made of Iroko-wood slats, and sandstone cobblestones define the borders of the carpet-like squares of stone laid in grass. The trees are Japanese maples.

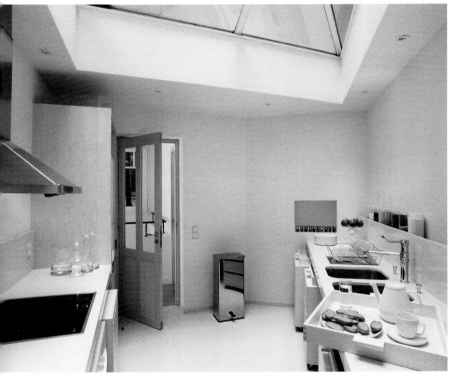

A large oak door
separates the kitchen
and dining area and a
"withdrawing" room in
which to rest.
Above: In the kitchen,
lots of light, stone and
sycamore wood.
Right: In the living
room, the serenity of
Asiatic wickerwork,
a paper lantern by
Noguchi and a low,
19th-century Chinese
lacquered table.

STROLLING THROUGH MONTMARTRE

1. À LA MÈRE DE FAMILLE

Few households today can boast cabinets as well stocked with such delicacies as we find here. Dedicated to the gourmet and the gourmand alike, this is a boutique devoted to the good life.
35, rue du Faubourg Montmartre, 75009.
Phone: +33 1 47 70 83 69.

2. XAVIER LENORMAND *A little bit of everything—at Lenormand's one finds furniture and decorative objects that he reassembles in his apartment. Floors full of treasures.*
11, rue de Provence, 75009.
Phone: +33 1 42 46 85 92.

3. LIBRAIRIE CHAMONAL

In this 100-year-old bookstore, exclusively devoted to books on travel and science, one can also find rare editions. For the expert and amateur alike.
5, rue Drouot, 75009.
Phone: +33 1 47 70 84 87.

4. SERGE PLANTUREUX *This eccentric with a mania for photography has his own museum; the annex is in the Galerie Vivienne. He's a collector and a dealer of a wide variety of curios.*
4, galerie Vivienne, 75002.
Phone: +33 1 53 29 92 00.

5. HÔTEL DROUOT *Visit here on a regular basis and waste plenty of time, as time can always be made up later. A truly exceptional establishment in France, this auction house is also unique in the world. The best items sit side by side with the worst, just like in the real world.*
9, rue Drouot, 75009.
Phone: +33 1 48 00 20 20.

6. THOMAS BOOG

Previously located in Passage Jouffroy (photo opposite), Thomas Boog, an expert on shells, recently opened a boutique on rue de Bourgogne, although more than just shells reside here.
52, rue de Bourgogne, 75007.
Phone: +33 1 43 17 30 03.

7. L'ACADÉMIE DE BILLARD

If for no other reason, one should visit this repository of green felt tables for the decor alone. It's essential.
84, rue de Clichy, 75009.
Phone: +33 1 48 78 32 85.

8. HUBERT DUCHEMIN *A tiny gallery where the owner has amassed 18th-century drawings and studies from different periods. Interesting to all knowledgeable collectors who are guaranteed to find something unusual.*
Passage Verdeau, 75009.

9. CLAUDE HUOT *This builder of fine furniture—whose den is frequented by the top antiques dealers—also restores paintings on wood.*
13, rue de Montyon, 75009.
Phone: +33 1 47 70 58 19.

10. ATELIER GUSTAVE MOREAU

For a long time it was Paris's best-kept secret. Rarely does one find a place like this where time stands still; where one can penetrate the universe of a great artist. The master of symbolism, Moreau left all his works to the city of Paris: paintings, drawings…everything exactly as it was at the moment of his death. An extraordinary place.
14, rue La Rochefoucauld, 75009.
Phone: +33 1 48 74 38 50.

11. ÉCOLE DE BRODERIE D'ART LESAGE

Having outlived the great silk embroiderers of the last century, François Lesage is looking toward the future and is nourishing new talent. This conservatory, whose items are both beautiful and finely crafted, is open to the public.
13, rue de la Grange-Batelière, 75009.
Phone: +33 1 48 24 14 20.

12. SOPHA *At Sopha, one finds the most beautiful and contemporary faucets and sinks. Here, hygiene has risen to an art form.*
44, rue Blanche, 75009.
Phone: +33 1 42 81 25 85.

1

5

7

9 10

2 3

4

6

8

11 12

THE RETURN OF THE ROMANTIC

The 9th arrondissement shelters mysteries of its own. Here, a young lawyer mixes neoclassic symmetry with a touch of modernism, along with the spirit of objects from Africa and Asia. When the weather is fine, he gives sophisticated dinners in his tiny jungle garden.

Left: Wide stripes painted on the wall contrast with the finer stripes of an 18th-century Gainsborough chair covered in velvet (Lelièvre). On the wall a pair of terracotta neo-Egyptian vases in the neoclassic style and a pair of late 18th-century engravings depicting Cupid with his swans. In the center, a work in ink by Jean-Marc Louis; the adjustable lamp on the right is by Philippe Starck. *Right:* In the entranceway-dining room, an early 19th-century plaster Bacchus finds its place in a niche formerly reserved for a stove. The whitewashed-gray double doors are trimmed in orange; a metal chandelier from the time of Charles X.

In the living room, the Empire style fraternizes with a bit of everything else: a tiger skin (from the Saint-Ouen flea market), a low, armless fireside chair by Jacob covered in ocelot skin, Louis Philippe-era armchairs inspired by the 17th century, a silk Asian-inspired lantern by Thomas Boog. On the Empire pedestal table, a chocolate-colored porcelain tea set by Utzschneider of Austria. The couch is in the Empire style; the 19th-century portraits depict Chinese dignitaries. The majority of the books were found bargain hunting at Béatrice Bablon.

A MAN OF MANY TALENTS

Above: In Christian Astuguevieille's kitchen, a table and a chair of braided hemp rope ingeniously designed by this decorator and innovator.
The wall's ocher tones, the monochromatic earthenware plates (by Creil and by Wedgewood), and the cupboard made of chestnut planks all harmonize with the natural color of hemp.

Left: Both functional and decorative, the cupboard provides the perfect display for a collection of plates. In the foreground, two slightly different chairs made of raw hemp rope.
Right: Against the back wall, a large sideboard made of cord was specifically designed to hold this collection of antique dishware.

A minimum of color and a sparsity of furniture serve to enhance the beautiful lines and high ceilings of this old artisan's studio.
Left: The counter is hewn out of a block of white stone, "Crème des Dunes." The faucets and sink are from Robinetterie Dornbracht. The table and two benches are made of heavy teak, the bookshelf is of oak —all stained a rich chocolate brown (design by Antonio Virga).
Below: The stained oak kitchen furniture was made to order and stained the same color as the parquet floors.

LESS IS MORE

Right: Diaphanous white curtains allow light to flood the room without obscuring the beautiful old frame windows. The salvaged radiator is from Le Radiateur en Fonte. The teak armchair was designed by Antonio Virga.
Below: In the bathroom the double-pedestal sink comes from the Grand Hôtel de Cabourg (La Baignoire Délirante). The tinted made-to-order oak cabinets swivel around to become mirrors and drawers.

This apartment, obviously inhabited by a collector, mixes 1940s design with neo-baroque furniture and interesting pieces of plaster.
Left: The 1950 dining room table is by Jean Royère. The paintings are by Pierre Buraglio and Jan Voss. The ceramic anthropomorphic vase is by Guéden. The floor lamp is by Poillerat. In the foreground, the coffee table made of mirror and bronze is by Arbus, all from the 1940s.
Below: On the mirrored bureau, a 19th-century porcelain bust by Thomas-Victor Sergent. The taboret is by Olivier Gagnère.

A LIGHT TOUCH

Right: The late-1930s straw screen on the left by Jean-Michel Frank is a centerpiece of the room. Two taborets from around 1990, by Gagnère, lend a touch of the contemporary. Hanging dramatically above the bed is a plaster-framed mirror attributed to Serge Roche; the gilded iron chair is by René Drouet; the pair of bedside tables are by André Arbus.
Below: In the bathroom, a wrought-iron easy chair from the 1980s by André Dubreuil. Two stucco mirrors with scallop shells are from Galerie Kartica.

Here we see the home environment of a collector who revels in the classic—souvenirs from travels abroad, classical statuettes, beautiful French and Swedish furniture from the 1930s and 1940s. *Left:* The 1930s armchairs and taborets are by Jean-Michel Frank; the vases are by Ernst Boiceau (from Galerie Eric Philippe), and the 1940s portrait is by Christian Bérard. *Below:* Atop the pale oak bookcase, *La Flûte de Pan* is by Lurçat; the reclining nude is by Eric Grate; the bronze lamp is by Arbus. Decor by Francis Roos.

THE COMFORT OF WOOD ALL AROUND

The study of a seasoned traveler and avid reader. *Left:* The 1920s mahogany desk inlaid with holly is from Galerie Eric Philippe; porcelain Sèvres vase from the 1940s; the lamp with the astrolabe base is by Gilbert Poillerat, as is the standing lamp in the corner of the library. *Right:* This room's centerpiece is a large, still life by Francis Jourdain. The Italian two-tiered library table from the 1940s is by Gio Ponti. A caned birch chair (Carl Malmstein); the rug is by Sue and Mare. Everything comes from Galerie Eric Philippe.

BEHIND THE SCENES AT THE HŌTEL DE CAMONDO

This recently restored home was named after its owner, Moïse de Camondo, who donated this property for a museum dedicated to the decorative arts of the 18th century. Although inspired by the architecture of the Trianon at Versailles, this beautiful house in the Plaine Monceau district had what was in 1900 considered an ultra-modern kitchen.

A well-known publisher lives here, at the other end of the book district. "This Haussmanian apartment, so often described in novels from the end of the 19th century, remains for me — once freed from its superfluous stuffiness — an ideal place to live," confesses the owner.

Right: In the living room, Roberto Bergero decorated the bookshelves in alternating patinas and Venetian stucco.
Below: In the dining room, a sienna patina gives the walls their buffed-gold look. The panels and resin wall lights were designed and painted by Bergero.

THE PARC MONCEAU REVEALED

Bill Pallot is a prominent specialist of 18th-century furniture and objects, an art historian and an associate of the great antiques dealer Didier Aaron. He's not exactly trying to create a "tasteful" decor in his home. Rather, he seeks shock value through an audacious mixture of styles. In his living room, the centerpiece is an oil painting by Jean-Michel Basquiat,

WHEN CONTEMPORARY ART MEETS GREAT OPULENCE

flanked by two magnificent 18th-century wall lights in gilded bronze designed for the duchess of Parma during the time of Louis XV. To the right of the chimney, a portrait by Antoyan. On the left, a dance mask from the Bobo tribe of Burkina-Faso. The couches, which date from the time of the Second Empire, are covered in embossed, silk velvet (Lelièvre).

Clockwise, from top left:
In front of a 1990s painting by Combas titled *Adam et Eve*, a 19th century clock, a Charles X candlestick holder with a reflecting screen; a 19th-century Austrian horn and the head of a cheetah made of papier-mâché. The 1940s table, decorated with lacquered panels, is from China.

In the entrance, a large rain drum from the Vanuatu tribe (Oceania). A Second Empire-patinated bronze griffin. Beneath a contemporary sculpture titled *Momie*, by Iommim, a remarkable 1750s armchair by the fine furniture maker Nicolas Heurtaut.

Right page: A neo-Gothic chair by George Alphonse Jacob, and an 1830 armchair with the original upholstery.

IN A BIBLIOPHILE'S HOME

For his personal library, José Alvarez, founder of French publishing company Editions du Regard, designed three levels of shelves for a 22-foot high room. Four French windows and wall lights attached to oak supports all help to brighten this room devoted to culture of all kinds. On the concrete floor, a lead sculpture by Anselm Kiefer. The blond-wood library table is from the 1930s. On the walls photographs by such varied artists as Gisèle Freund, Rogi-André, Rodchenko, and Helmut Newton.

THE PINNACLE OF ART DECO

Designed by architect Boileau in 1925, the Prunier restaurant was rescued and restored by Pierre Bergé and transformed into a fish restaurant whose specialty is caviar from the Aquitaine region of France. The romantic, dusky atmosphere will no doubt play a part in its success.

Clockwise from top left: The gilded art deco wooden panel evokes a mysterious undersea world.

The marble staircase is inlayed with onyx, sintered glass, and gold leaf.

At the end of the bar, a bronze Breton fisherman who fished in Iceland, reminds one of the writer Pierre Loti and his work, a contemporary of Emile Prunier and the author of *Fishermen of Iceland.*

A view of the bar, left intact from the days when Prunier was considered one of the most elegant restaurants of the 16th arrondissement — a time when few restaurants existed in the area.

Right page: On the double doors, the sea horse motif etched in glass is the restaurant's trademark. The restaurant is registered with the Bureau of Historic Monuments.

Sculptor Hubert
Le Gall designed this
space to accommodate
items from the 1930s
and 1940s that the
owners had assembled
in their 16th-
arrondissement
townhouse.
Left: Between
two windows, a work
by Tamara de Lempicka.
In the foreground,
furniture from the
1940s (Christian
Sapet) on an
art deco-style rug.
Below: Closely hung
works with a Picasso
drawing in the center
suspended from
a bronze leaf.

A COLLECTOR'S
HOME

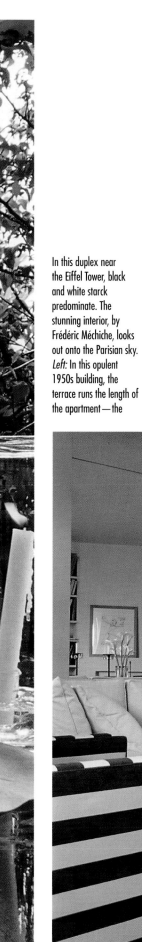

In this duplex near the Eiffel Tower, black and white starck predominate. The stunning interior, by Frédéric Méchiche, looks out onto the Parisian sky. *Left:* In this opulent 1950s building, the terrace runs the length of the apartment—the terrace furniture was designed by Frédéric Méchiche for Hugonet. *Below:* In the austere living room, a cauldron-shaped sculpture by Eric Schmidt; the striped sofas and the day bed are covered in raw linen. In the background, to the right, is the dining area.

A DUPLEX'S WHITE MAGIC

Below: In this bedroom, the slipcovers are made of white linen (First Time).
Right: The kitchen's black-and-white motif matches the living room. The mosaic checkerboard flooring is made of antiqued marble. The ceiling is painted in black lacquer; the kitchen range and hood and the work areas are of stainless steel (Gaggenau). The wall lights are from the 1950s, the chair is by Bertoïa (Knoll), and the black dishes are by Calvin Klein. On the counter, a ceramic work by the American artist Sol Lewitt.

This triplex, which overlooks the Bois de Boulogne, makes use of transparency, natural tones and sparsity. Julia Errera, a real estate agent, entrusted Yves Taralon with the redecoration of her triplex.

GOOD TASTE, PLAIN AND SIMPLE

Left: "City" couches (B et B), drapes by Rubelli, a wool rug by Lauer, all beautiful shades of white.
Above: In this passageway through which one is obliged to pass when going from the kitchen to the living room, an oak bar designed by Yves Taralon.
Right: The wrought iron handrail along the staircase is by Olivier Gagnère.

243

Right: In Julia's room, the bed is set at a diagonal. The linens are from Postel-Vinay; Egée lamps (Artoff), teacup by Bernardaud; the painting is by Claude Lepoitevin.
Left: The etched-glass doors are dotted with the same gilded bronze as these specially designed door handles.
Below: A view of the bathroom, as seen through a door of corded ash. The sink is by Philippe Starck.

LET THERE BE LIGHT

Bright light and raw materials are the theme for this loft-like duplex apartment. The living room's pine plank floors are painted lead white. The 1925 cupboard is made of burled walnut; the pillar sculpture to the far left is from the Dogon tribe of Mali (galerie de Monbrison); The closet doors and table, of the African Fraké-wood, were made to order. The armchair is by Pescatore; the kitchen chairs are made of zinc (Fenêtre sur Cour). The walls are covered in flat white paint (Emery et Cie).

In the entrance,
a large bookcase made
of Fraké-wood covers
the wall. The polished
concrete staircase leads
to an open bedroom.
A glass wall allows
for magnificent
unobstructed views
of the rooftops.

the MARCHĒ AUX PUCES *and the* SUBURBS

Speaking of the most famous of all the flea markets…it was previously called the Saint-Ouen flea market; today it is known as the flea market at Clignancourt. In its first iteration, it referred to a village on the outskirts of Paris. In the second, it goes by the name of one of the numerous "gates" to the city that once allowed outsiders through the city's encircling wall. Clignancourt is at the city limits, where the metro line ends. For a long time, between this gate and the village of Saint-Ouen, it was a wasteland. As late as the 1960s, gypsies, rag pickers and junk peddlers camped there. They played the guitar, burned unidentifiable debris and sold the pitiful belongings of people who had reached the end of their wretched lives to others who were as destitute as they (but for the fact they still had their lives!). After some haggling, these buyers would purchase such necessities as a tabletop gas stove or a chamber pot.

"Cleanliness is the luxury of the poor—the rich, go ahead and be dirty," wrote André Breton in his first Surrealist Manifesto. The original members of the Surrealist movement, displaying through their art the tenets Breton laid down in his manifesto, went bargain hunting in the area between Clignancourt and Saint-Ouen for wicker mannequins, nightingale cages, umbrellas and sewing machines. Soon it had a certain bohemian caché and photographs from the late 1930s show celebrities such as Bérard, Kochno, Henri Sauguet and Christian Dior strolling through the cast-off remnants of this world, drawing inspiration from objects they found there. It was called the "flea" market because there was always the chance that you'd get some.

Fifty years later, it's still called the flea market. Flea markets are a metaphor for our own lives—they represent what is lost and gained; as characterized by the famous phrase "one man's trash is another man's riches." Browsers always leave with something that they hadn't been looking for. People speak with familiarity to merchants who, everyone supposes, are cheating you. And perhaps one day, if they do well enough here, these merchants will be able to open up some fancy

the MARCHĒ AUX PUCES

establishment in the Beaux Quartiers area. For the real miracle of the flea market is seeing such an enormous number of people pass through at such a furious pace, exchanging money (and considerable sums, at that) in the absence of any commercial controls.

The flea market could have become just another chic, trendy place—like the Village Suisse, or the original second-hand stores around the Place Furstenberg. The secret to its success is that it remained a place where it was possible to find just about anything—and something for everyone. Not unlike days long past when at the openings of Jean Genet's plays, socialites mingled with pimps. The contrasts can be stark: from antiques once passed down through generations to cell phones; here, we find mirrors; over there, second-hand smoking jackets. It's for this very reason that we love our flea markets. They are veritable showplaces that represent the evolution of a species that faithfully follows the formula of a famous Nobel Prize winner: "Chance, and necessity."

As the name indicates, the suburbs begin where the city ends—not a very enticing description. Although long a source of numerous problems, they are also the source of many services. Up until the 1960s, suburban produce farmers and florists still drove to Paris in their horse-drawn carts to deliver their wares. After that, developers came in and took over most of the farms and orchards—it had become necessary to house the masses of people who flocked to Paris for jobs or whatever draws people to the city.

As mentioned earlier, Paris, over the centuries, grew outward from its center at the Ile de la Cité (then known as Lutèce) in a spiraling fashion, expanding as its fortifications expanded. Just beyond the final outer walls, built by Minister Thiers between 1841 and 1844, lay what was referred to as "la zone." That term, which became part of the popular vernacular, came to describe something very specific: neither the city, the country, nor the suburbs, but a place of upheaval and deterioration.

In the past, this area outside the city walls supposedly allowed our courageous defenders to shoot their enemies out in this open area like rabbits. Although the countryside has never been very far away from Paris, "la zone"—although topographically closer—is still considered today, some 150 years later, far removed from the center of Parisian life. Situated for the most part to the north and to the east of Paris, those who lived there, bohemians and the destitute, constructed their shantytowns after the war with whatever fate provided them. Little by little, these shantytowns were replaced by moderately priced housing projects and stadiums, or were left as green open spaces. Beyond "la zone" lie the suburbs. Without a doubt, "la zone" represents the future of greater Paris.

and the SUBURBS

Beyond the beltway, which was built around the city during de Gaulle's administration, a variety of communities have emerged, each one different in character and each with its own individual charm—unless ravaged by city planners. But Parisians who are familiar only with the Neuilly region or the Marché aux Puces should be reminded that our suburbs too are worth knowing and should be recognized as such; like Levallois, Asnières, Issy-les-Moulineaux, Garches, Saint-Cloud, Saint-Mandé and Charenton.

The people who live there are often former Parisians who decided to leave because of the exorbitant price of housing, because the air was cleaner outside of the capital or because their families were growing and they needed more space. Today Paris is populated by the rich, the elderly and by singles (who now make up more than 50% of the population). The rest of the city is mostly offices and boutiques.

These words from a famous song, "It isn't love, it's only its suburbs," illustrate the Parisian contempt for their suburbs. But in a truly French paradox, these bucolic regions outside of Paris's "walls" seem to nevertheless attract city-dwellers. The tradition of fleeing the miasma and crush of the city on beautiful Sunday afternoons dates back to the 18th century and still continues today—Parisians went there to row boats and fill the country bistros.

Rich in cellars, attics, arbors and borders of flowers, these homes have become the dream of the new bourgeois-bohemian set whose ancestors came from the nearby countryside themselves. As of late, young couples have taken to dreaming of owning their own English cottage or a small farmhouse, or joining a retreat for artists and unrecognized composers...not to mention the seaside resorts reachable by Parisian train lines.

Things from the 1970s that were once considered kitsch, though still considered tacky, are now viewed as charming. We don't throw away grandmother's armoire, or her cuckoo clock, or even her old metal box for bouillon cubes. Everything has its purpose, and its price. With time, all things change and evolve and what could not have been imagined ten short years ago is now all the rage. Flea markets attest to that fact as much as the evolution of the suburbs: Tomorrow is always another day.

AN ANTIQUES DEALER'S SHOWCASE HOUSE

Having left Paris to live close to the flea market, Annick Clavier, who deals in antiques and flea-market finds, operates her business every weekend from her picturesque suburban home swathed in greenery on rue Paul-Bert in Saint-Ouen. The Virginia creeper is her only inviolate secret. *Right:* The garden where everything is for sale.

Annick Clavier's
basement serves as
a typically French
kitchen, dining room
and living room.
Above: In a corner
of the dining area,
exposed brick has
been painted white.
Right: The corner
kitchen is separated
from the living room
by a wooden counter.
In front of the couch
(First Time), a pair
of English leather
armchairs.

In this living room,
a portrait of a 1930s
pugilist and neoclassic
leather chairs.
The pine paneling
was found in a
salvage shop.

A TRIPLEX WITH CONFIDENCE

Christian Sapet,
one of the most popular
antiques dealers of
the Paul Bert flea
market, maintains
that he was only being
practical when
he elected to buy
for his weekend
getaway this big old
three-story house.
Left: Below the second
floor staircase, a small
bedroom-sitting room.
Above the Directoire-
style bed on the left,
a mirror gives
the illusion of being
in the crosshairs.

Above, right: In this bachelor's bedroom, a wrought iron bed covered by a 19th-century quilt from Provence. The bookshelves are archival shelving. The walls are paneled in raw wood planks whitewashed in Blanc d'Espagne.
Below, right: The bathroom sink comes from a luxury hotel and dates back to the turn of the century. An ultra-flat radiator serves to camouflage the bathtub.
Right page: Louvered shutters filter the light from above falling on this loggia. The bronze sculpture is by Hiquili; the 1910 oil painting is by Paul Vera; the 1910 table is by Serrurier-Bovy and the 1950 seats are by Subes.

AN OASIS UNDER THE VIADUCT

In the suburbs, amidst a tangle of vegetation, some strange islets can be found, like this unusual sheltered villa near a railroad track in Issy-les-Moulineaux. *Left page*: A lovely view overlooking the willow trees in a garden configured by Alain-Frédéric Bisson. *Left*: A log table by David Hicks; the "log" pottery is by Lopez. Everything here enhances the sense of calm, even the dog relaxing under an open window.

Above: In this corner kitchen, a painted butcher block was turned into a console; the candlestick lamps have been electrified. The screen is covered in damask (Pierre Frey). *Right*: In this house in Issy, the kitchen-dining room has a neo-Gothic mantelpiece. Between two windows, a rustic sideboard from the 17th century. The chairs are from the Arts and Crafts period, and the carpet is in needlepoint.

Above: A romantic bedroom setting with a faux leopard rug (Casa Lopez), and a pair of mirrored mahogany armoires in the Louis Philippe style. A French quilted bedspread (Blanc d'Ivoire).
Right: In the living room a three-sided ottoman couch in the style of Louis XV is flanked by two unusual painted metal shelves resembling Christmas trees, and a rug with floral designs (all from Casa Lopez). A rustic Italian table (Vivement Jeudi).

Just minutes away from the bustling French capital, a calm, verdant enclave dominates the heights of Meudon with its very British style of charm. Nad Laroche and her architect husband moved there some 20 years ago in order to raise their three daughters and they've never regretted it.
Below: In the entrance, the marble flooring is from Carrara, Italy. The painted console table is in the Directoire style.

ENGLISH STYLE AT THE GATES OF PARIS

Left: In this half-paneled dining room, the ebony table is circled by Arne Jacobsen chairs (1950s). The toile de Jouy wallpaper in manganese is by Braquenié; the chandelier is from the 19th century.
Below: The kitchen opens onto a winter garden. Living in the suburbs, one can take advantage of the bounty of both city and country.

Right. In the bedroom-
cum-library, skillfully
ordered disorder.
The 19th-century
furniture is mahogany;
the Nad Laroche
tapestry is after a
design by Paul Klee;
the chairs are English,
and the jumble of
objects, many bestowed
as gifts, are testimony
to numerous friendships.
Below. In the bathroom,
fruitwood and marble
add distinction.

Photographs by:

Alexandre Bailhache: pp. 164-165 *(ph. 4, 6, 7, 10, 11, 12)*, 192, 194, 200-201 *(ph. 1–6 and 8–12)*.
Joseph Benita: p. 186 *(ph. 11)*.
Guy Bouchet: p. 187 *(ph. 12)*, back cover *(4th row ph. 3)*.
Gilles de Chabaneix: pp. 48–51, 88–91, 162-163, 242–245, 270–275, back cover *(4th row ph. 4)*.
Stephen Clément: pp. 210–213, 246–249, back cover *(1st row ph. 3, 3rd row ph. 2)*.
Xavier Coton: pp. 16, 18-19 *(ph. 1, 3–8)*, 26 *(ph. 1)*, 28 *(center)*, 60-61 *(ph. 1, 3, 13)*, 78-79, 109 *(ph. 5)*, 126-127, 131 *(ph. 12)*, 136-137 *(ph. 9, 10)*, 145 *(ph. 8)*, 187 *(ph. 10, 13)*, 195 *(ph. 8)*, back cover *(3rd row ph. 3)*.
Vera Cruz: pp. 254–259, back cover *(1st row ph. 1)*.
Pierre-Olivier Deschamps: pp. 174-175, 200 *(ph. 7)*, 252 *(bottom left)*, 253 *(top left)*.
Pierre-Olivier Deschamps/Vu: pp. 61 *(ph. 8)*, 82-83, 97 *(ph. 2)*, 108 *(ph. 2)*, 136 *(ph. 6)*, 145 *(ph. 11)*, 187 *(ph. 3, 4, 5)*, 195 *(ph. 6)*, 230-231, back cover *(4th row ph. 1)*.
Deyrolle: pp. 76 *(top left and bottom right)*, 77.
Jacques Dirand: pp. 46-47, 64–67, 92–95, 109 *(ph. 9)*, 118-119, 138–141, 196–199, 208-209, 214–217, 238–241, back cover *(1st row ph. 2)*.
Alain Gelberger: p. 97 *(ph. 8)*.
G. Guérin: p. 253 *(bottom right)*.
Patrice de Grandry: pp. 116-117.
Marianne Haas: endpapers *(ph. 2)*, pp. 26-27 *(ph. 4–11)*, 32–39, 40-41 *(ph. 3, 5, 6, 9, 10)*, 42–45, 68–71, 76 *(top right and bottom left)*, 84–87, 96 *(ph. 4, 5)*, 98-99, 114-115, 120-121, 128-129, 130-131 *(ph. 1, 2, 4, 6–8, 10, 13)*, 136-137 *(ph. 1, 8, 12)*, 154–157, 164-165 *(ph. 1, 3, 5, 8, 9)*, 226–229, 236-237, back cover *(2nd row ph. 2, 4th row ph. 2)*.
Pierre-Laurent Hahn: pp. 160-161.
Olivier Hallot: pp. 144 *(ph. 5)*, 186-187 *(ph. 2, 6, 7)*.
Éric d'Hérouville: endpapers *(except ph. 2)*, 58-59, 61 *(ph. 2)*, 136 *(ph. 5)*, 144-145 *(ph. 1, 2, 4, 6, 7 10)*, 186 *(ph. 9)*.
Noëlle Hoeppe: pp. 137 *(ph. 2)*, 224-225.
Seline Keller: pp. 132-135.
Vincent Knapp: pp. 104-107, back cover *(2nd row ph. 1)*.
Joël Laiter: pp. 52-53, 80-81, 202–207.
Guillaume de Laubier: cover, pp. 18 *(ph. 2)*, 20–25, 27 *(ph. 13)*, 40 *(ph. 1)*, 41 *(ph. 11)*, 54–57, 61 *(ph. 6, 11, 12)*, 72–75, 96-97 *(ph. 1, 3, 6, 7, 13)*, 102-103, 108-109 *(ph. 1, 4, 6, 7, 8)*, 110-111, 112-113, 124, 131 *(ph. 3, 9, 11)*, 137 *(ph. 13, 14)*, 146-151, 152-153, 158-159, 166–169, 170–173, 180-181, 182–185, 186-187 *(ph. 1, 8)*, 195 *(ph. 5)*, 218–221, 222-223, 260–263, back cover *(2nd row ph. 3, 3rd row ph. 1)*.
Hervé Lorgeré: p. 41 *(ph. 12)*.
Nicolas Mathéus: pp. 28 *(top and bottom)*, 28-29, 30-31, 188–191, 232–235.
Philippe Matsas: p. 195 *(ph. 7)*.
Éric Morin: pp. 142-143.
François Mouriès: pp. 26 *(ph. 2, 3, 12)*, 40-41 *(ph. 2, 4, 7, 8)*, 60 *(ph. 4, 5, 7, 9, 10)*, 96-97 *(ph. 9, 10, 11)*, 131 *(ph. 5)*, 136-137 *(ph. 3, 4, 7, 11)*, 145 *(ph. 3, 12)*.
Jacques Primois: pp. 176–179.
M. Renaudeau/Hoaqui: p. 252 *(top left)*.
Ivan Terestchenko: pp. 264–269.
Vincent Thibert: p. 97 *(ph. 12)*.
Gilles Trillard: pp. 62-63, 100-101, 108 *(ph. 3)*, 122-123, 144 *(ph. 9)*.
Buss Wojtek/Hoaqui: pp. 252 *(center)*, 253 *(top right)*.
A. Wolf/Explorer: p. 250.

Style by:

Alexandra d'Arnoux: pp. 224-225.

François Baudot: pp. 36–39, 58-59, 84–87, 98-99, 102-103, 108 *(ph. 1)*, 174-175, 187 *(ph. 3, 4, 5)*.

Marie-Claire Blanckaert: cover, pp. 20–25, 32–35, 46-47, 54–57, 62-63, 64–67, 68–71, 72–75, 100, 101, 104-107, 108 *(ph. 1, 3, 4)*, 110-111, 112-113, 122-123, 128-129, 138–141, 144 *(ph. 9)*, 146–151, 158-159, 160-161, 162-163, 164 *(ph. 1, 9)*, 176–179, 180-181, 182–185, 187 *(ph. 8)*, 196–199, 214–217, 222-223, 226–229, 238–241, 242–245, 254–259, 264–269, 270–275, back cover *(1st row ph. 2, 2nd row ph. 1)*.

Marie-Claire Blanckaert and Gérard Pussey: pp. 182-185.

Barbara Bourgois: pp. 132-135, 144 *(ph. 5)*.

Jérôme Coignard: pp. 166–169.

Françoise Delbecq: pp. 152-153.

Françoise Delbecq and Françoise Labro: pp. 118-119.

Laurence Dougier: pp. 188–191, 232–235.

Marie-Claude Dumoulin: pp. 88–91.

Armel Ferroudj-Begou: pp. 116-117.

Inès Heugel: pp. 164 *(ph. 5)*, 165 *(ph. 3, 8)*, back cover *(4th row ph. 2)*.

Marie Kalt: pp. 92–95, 164-165 *(ph. 2, 4, 6, 7, 10, 11, 12)*, 192, 194, 200-201 *(ph. 1–6 and 8–12)*, 208-209.

Marie Kalt and Gérard Pussey: pp. 260–263.

Françoise Labro: pp. 154–157.

Marie-Maud Levron: pp. 136 *(ph. 5)*, 144-145 *(ph. 4 and 6)*.

Catherine Mamet: pp. 210–213, back cover *(1st row ph. 3)*.

Franck Maubert: p. 195 *(ph. 6)*.

Nathalie Nort: pp. 186-187 *(ph. 2, 6, 7)*.

Marie-Paule Pellé: pp. 52-53.

Olivia Phélip and Monique Duveau: pp. 80-81.

Marie-France Pochna: pp. 218–221.

Misha de Potestad: pp. 108-109 *(ph. 6, 7, 8)*, 136 *(ph. 6)*.

Gérard Pussey: pp. 114-115.

Isabelle Rosanis: pp. 246–249, back cover *(3rd row ph. 2)*.

Catherine Scotto: pp. 97 *(ph. 8, 12)*, 142-143, 202–207, 236-237.

Elsa Simon: pp. 48–51, back cover *(4th row ph. 4)*.

Sylvie Tardrew: pp. 18 *(ph. 2)*, 27 *(ph. 13)*, 40 *(ph. 1)*, 41 *(ph. 11)*, 61 *(ph. 6, 11, 12)*, 96-97 *(ph. 1, 3, 6, 7, 13)*, 124, 131 *(ph. 3 and 11)*, 137 *(ph. 13 and 14)*.

Laure Verchère and Olivier Chapel-Stick: p. 200 *(ph. 7)*.

Laure Verchère: pp. 26-27 *(ph. 2–12)*, 28–31, 40-41 *(ph. 2–10, 12)*, 42 à 45, 60-61 *(ph. 2, 4, 5, 7, 9, 10)*, 76 *(top right and bottom left)*, 82-83, 96-97 *(ph. 2, 4, 5, 9, 10, 11)*, 109 *(ph. 9)*, 130-131 *(ph. 1, 2, 4–8, 10, 13)*, 136-137 *(ph. 1, 3, 4, 7, 8, 11, 12)*, 144-145 *(ph. 1–3, 7, 10–12)*, 170–173, 186 *(ph. 9)*, 230-231, 252 *(bottom left)*, 253 *(top left and bottom right)*, back cover *(2nd row ph. 2 and 3, 4th row ph. 1)*.

Olivier de Vleeschouwer: p. 61 *(ph. 8)*.

Agnès Waendendries: p. 137 *(ph. 2)*.

Clara Whitebus: p. 186 *(ph. 1)*.

Claire Wilson: pp. 120-121.

Elle Décoration (France) and *Elle Decor* (U.S.) are both imprints of the Hachette Filipacchi group.

The content of this book was taken solely from *Elle Décoration* and appeared only in France.

We would like to thank the owners, decorators, architects, institutions and hotels that welcomed *Elle Décoration* collaborators for this publication:

José Alvarez - Christian Astuguevieille - Dominique Bénard-Dépalle - Pierre Bergé - Roberto Bergero - Alexandre Biaggi - Alain-Frédéric Bisson - Thomas Boog - Laurent Bourgois - Frédéric Castaing - Stéphanie Cauchoix - Annick Clavier - Agnès Comar - Patrice Corbin - Jean-Louis Costes - Robert Couturier - Nathalie Decoster - Alain Demachy - Francis Dorléans - Mrs Ehringer - Julia Errera - Monic Fisher – Jacques Garcia - Yves Gastou - Anne Gayet - Didier Gomez - François Joseph Graf - Jacques Grange – Jean-Pierre Grédy - Dominique Guéroult (Deyrolle) - Yves and Michèle Halard - Anouska Hempel - Michelle Joubert - Aïcha Kouhail (Annick Goutal Parfums) - Karl Lagerfeld - Nad Laroche - Roland Le Bevillon - Hubert Le Gall - Jacques Leguennec - Jean-Paul Leymarie - Véronique Lopez - Serge Lutens - Frédéric Méchiche - Catherine Memmi - Joëlle Mortier Vallat - Alain Ozanne - Bill Pallot - Alberto Pinto - Marie-France Pochna - Dany Postel-Vinay - Andrée Putman - Roxane Rodriguez - Jean de Rohan-Chabot - Francis Roos - Jean-Marie Rossi - Yves Saint Laurent - Christian Sapet - Maurice Savinel - Yves Taralon - Françoise Verny - Hervé Vermesch - Tino Zervudachi.

Blanc d'Ivoire, the musée Camondo, Flamant, l'Hôtel, Ladurée, the Opéra Garnier, Prunier, the Ritz, Vuitton.

And to all of them who wished to stay anonymous.

Color separation: Offset Publicité.
Printed in France by Clerc.